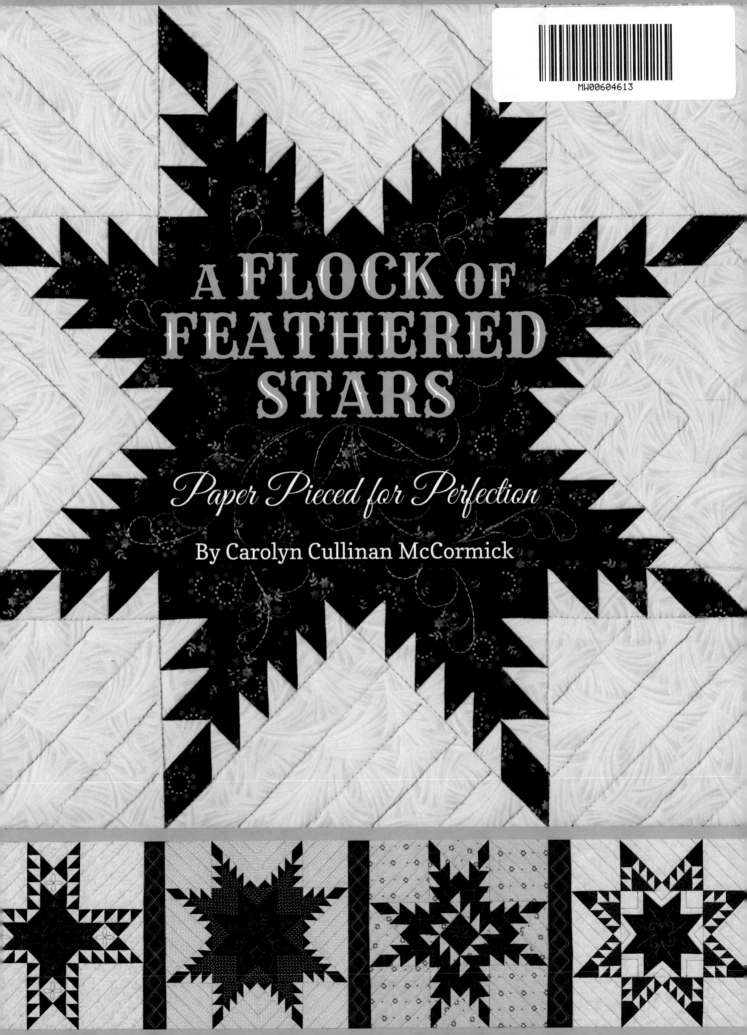

A FLOCK OF FEATHERED STARS

Paper Pieced for Perfection

By Carolyn Cullinan McCormick

A FLOCK OF FEATHERED STARS

Paper Pieced for Perfection

By Carolyn Cullinan McCormick

Editor: Edie McGinnis
Book Designer: Bob Deck
Photography: Aaron T. Leimkuehler
Illustrations: Eric Sears
Technical Editor: Jane Miller
Production Assistance: Jo Ann Groves

Published by:

Kansas City Star Books
1729 Grand Blvd.
Kansas City, Missouri, USA 64108

First edition, first printing
ISBN: 978-1-61169-080-4

Library of Congress Control Number: 2012955329

Printed in the United States of America by Walsworth Publishing Co., Marceline, MO

To order copies, call StarInfo at (816) 234-4242 and say "Books."

FALLING LEAVES TABLE RUNNER

Made and Quilted by
Carolyn Cullinan McCormick

DEDICATION

To my friend and "sister of the heart," Diane Donnelly. I am so blessed to have you in my life. Thanks for taking me under your wing so many, many years ago and getting me so excited about quilting!

- -

ACKNOWLEDGEMENTS

Words cannot express how grateful I am to my wonderful husband Larry … he is simply an amazing husband, father and grandfather. I love you very much!

Thank you so much to all who gave up their precious time to test the blocks. I really appreciate you more than you know. Aunt Betty's Star, Marilyn Vap, Castle Rock, Colo.; California Star, Carol Netwal, Castle Rock, Colo.; Chestnut Burr, Wendy Kay, Castle Rock, Colo.; Feathered Edge Star, Carol Bonetti, Castle Rock, Colo.; Feathered Star No. 1, Jan Korytkowski, Castle Rock, Colo.; Feathered Star No. 2, Jan Rickter, Castle Rock, Colo.; Feathered Star No. 3, Jeannette Davis, Castle Rock, Colo.; Feathered Star No. 4, Diane Donnelly, Bozeman, Mont.; Feathered Star No. 5, Polly Somers, Sedalia, Colo.; Feathered Star No. 6, LouAnn McGraw, Castle Rock, Colo.; Feathered Star Variation, Jennie Miller, Castle Rock, Colo.; Feathered Star, Finley, Connie Stewart, Castle Rock, Colo.; Morning Star, Jean V. Brabec, Slashed Star, Kathy Hannah, Castle Rock, Colo.; Star-of-Chamblie, Marie Llanes, Castle Rock, Colo.; The Hour Glass, The Twinkling Star, Ginny Rafferty, Castle Rock, Colo.

Also, many thanks to Carol Netwal for attaching the binding to the test block quilt.

Doug Weaver, thank you for giving me the opportunity to do another book for The Kansas City Star … I am so very grateful for the opportunity to work with the staff at The Star.

I am so fortunate to have amazing people working on this book. First and foremost, I want to thank my editor, Edie McGinnis, who is not only a fabulous editor but also my friend. Eric Sears did an amazing job with all of the patterns … feathered stars are not easy to draft. Technical editor, Jane Miller, made sure all of the measurements are correct. Thanks to page designer, Bob Deck, for making the book look so wonderful! Thanks also go to Jo Ann Groves for her production work on the photos.

I would like to thank the following companies that supplied fabrics and batting for this book: Lissa Alexander, Moda Fabrics; Dan Weidmueller, Newcastle Fabrics; and Dawn Pereira, Warm Company for the batting.

Thanks also to the long-arm quilters that did such a marvelous job quilting the quilts, Carol Willey with Willey Nice Quilts from Castle Rock, Colo. and Susan Batemann with Canterberry Quilts from Parker, Colo. You are amazing!

FEATHERED FRIENDS

Carol Netwal, Castle Rock, Colo.; Marilyn Vap, Castle Rock, Colo.; Wendy Kay, Castle Rock, Colo.;
Carol Bonetti, Castle Rock, Colo.; Jan Korytkowski, Castle Rock, Colo.; Jan Rickter, Castle Rock, Colo.;
Jeannette Davis, Castle Rock, Colo.; Diane Donnelly, Bozeman, Mont.; Polly Somers, Sedalia, Colo.;
LouAnn McGraw, Castle Rock, Colo.; Jennie Miller, Castle Rock, Colo.; Connie Stewart, Castle Rock,
Colo.; Jean V. Brabec, Kathy Hannah, Castle Rock, Colo.; Marie Llanes, Castle Rock, Colo.;
Ginny Rafferty, Castle Rock, Colo.
Quilted by Susan Batemann, Parker, Colo. Binding attached by Carol Netwall, Castle Rock, Colo.

Carolyn Cullinan McCormick currently lives in Franktown, Colorado, which is just a hop, skip and a jump from Denver, with her husband, Larry. They have a son, Ryan, and a daughter, Jennifer. Ryan and his wife, Megan, have two little girls, McKenna Carolyn who is 4 and Kate Elizabeth who is 1. Jennifer and her husband Anthony have a son, Lincoln Larry who is 3 months old.

Carolyn started to quilt in 1985 when she and her family moved to Bozeman, Montana. There she worked and taught a variety of quilting and craft classes at The Patchworks from 1987 to 1995. In 1995, she invented the Add-A-Quarter ruler to make rotary cutting of templates easier. The Add-A-Quarter has now become a standard tool for paper piecing.

Carolyn has invented other tools as well: The Add-An-Eighth, Add-Three-Eighths and the Add-Enough are more of the gadgets that make life much easier for quilters. You can see all her products and books at **www.addaquarter.com**.

TABLE OF CONTENTS

INTRODUCTION

I have always been so amazed by feathered star quilts, especially the quilts that were made in the 1800s. The quilter from the 1800s did not have the "tools" of today. They made those fabulous quilts using a template made of whatever was available along with their fabric, needle, thread and scissors.

My dear friend, Diane Donnelly, and I share a passion for old quilts. In 2009, she gave me a book called *Quilts Their Story and How to Make Them*, written by Marie D. Webster in 1915. Seeing how excited I was with that book, she gave me another later that year called *Romance of the Patchwork Quilt in America* written by Carrie A. Hall and Rose G. Kretsinger in 1935. That was all the inspiration I needed to write a book on how to paper piece feathered stars. (That is the only way to make a feathered star quilt … right?)

Some of the designs in the books used pieces that finished at 1" or less, and I have to admit some of them were quite a challenge to draft. I wanted to get as many designs as possible into one quilt along with a border block (I had to have a border block) that I had seen on one of the quilts without making the book so big you couldn't lift it.

I hope you like the selection of feathered star blocks I have chosen to include. Some of the blocks you may have seen before but others are designs that I think will be a pleasant surprise.

Enjoy!

Carolyn Cullinan McCormick

STARS OF THE NIGHT

Quilt Size: 84" Square

Made by Carolyn Cullinan McCormick
Quilted by Carol Willey, Castle Rock, Colo.

SUPPLY LIST

Fabrics:
Center Block and Pieced Border:
- ◊ 1 ⅜ yds. Light
- ◊ 1 yd. Dark

Blocks and Pieced Border:
- ◊ ¾ yd. each of 16 Lights
- ◊ ½ yd. each of 16 Darks

Blocks, Borders, Sashing, Corner Triangles, Cornerstones and Binding:
- ◊ 4 ½ yds. Solid Black

Backing:
- ◊ 7 ¾ yds. 45" wide

Batting:
- ◊ 2 ½ yds. 90" wide

Before making copies of all the feathered star patterns, cut the binding off the book so the patterns will lay flat. Some copy machines may distort the pattern, so always check for accuracy.

Other Supplies:
- ◊ Add-A-Quarter
- ◊ Scotch Permanent Double-Sided Tape
- ◊ Rotary Cutter and Mat
- ◊ Tweezers
- ◊ Rulers for Rotary Cutting
- ◊ Straight Pins
- ◊ Sewing Machine / Extra Needles
- ◊ Thread
- ◊ Paper Scissors
- ◊ Basic Sewing Supplies
- ◊ Iron and Ironing Board
- ◊ Muslin to Protect Ironing Board

Suggestions for cutting fabric pieces:
When it is necessary to use only a few pieces from a strip, start with the widest strip, cut the largest pieces first then cut the next size. There is no need to cut a strip for each size when only 1 to 4 pieces are needed. Tips for perfect, feathered stars:

1. Trim paper patterns ⅛" from the trimming line (dotted line) before starting to sew on fabrics.

2. Sew a scant ¼" - not on the line but along the line on the right side.

3. Sew the units together with the most points on top. This will allow you to see the points so they will not be cut off.

FEATHERED STAR NO. 4

BLOCK SIZE: 12" Finished

Cutting Instructions:

NOTE: *Some strips may have fabric left over. Measurements were figured on 42" wide fabric.*

From the light fabric, cut:

1 – 5 ¼" x 10 ½" strip. Cut the strip into 2 – 5 ¼" squares. Cut each square from corner to corner once on the diagonal to make triangles.

1 – 4 ½" x 18" strip. Cut the strip into 4 – 4 ½" squares.

1 – 4" x 8" strip. Cut the strip into 2 – 4" squares. Cut each square from corner to corner once on the diagonal to make triangles.

1 – 2 ½" strip. Cut the strip into 14 – 2 ½" squares. Cut each square from corner to corner once on the diagonal to make triangles.

From the dark fabric, cut:

1 – 4 ¾" square.

1 – 3 ½" x 14" strip. Cut the strip into 4 – 3 ½" squares. Cut each square from corner to corner once on the diagonal to make triangles.

1 – 2 ½" strip. Cut the strip into 16 – 2 ½" squares. Cut each square from corner to corner once on the diagonal to make triangles.

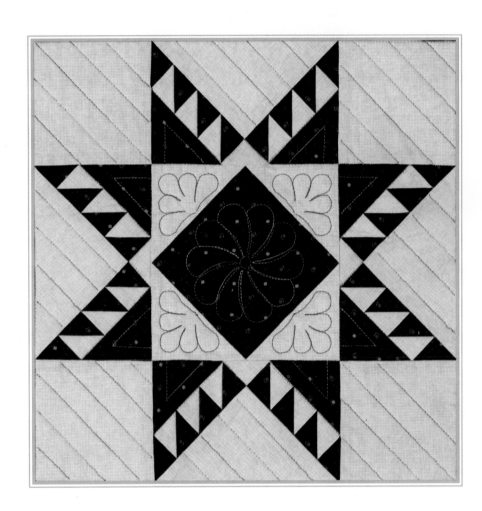

	Fabric	Position	Size	
Unit A – Make 4				
	Dark	1,3,5,7	2 ½" x 2 ½"	◹
	Light	2,4,6	2 ½" x 2 ½"	◹
	Dark	8	3 ½" x 3 ½"	◹
	Light	9	5 ¼" x 5 ¼"	◹
Unit B – Make 4				
	Dark	1,3,5,7	2 ½" x 2 ½"	◹
	Light	2,4,6,8	2 ½" x 2 ½"	◹
	Dark	9	3 ½" x 3 ½"	◹
Unit C – Make 4				
	Light	1	4 ½" x 4 ½"	
Unit D – Make 1				
	Dark	1	4 ¾" x 4 ¾"	
	Light	2,3,4,5	4" x 4"	◹

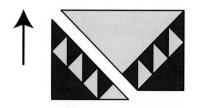

Sew units A to units B.

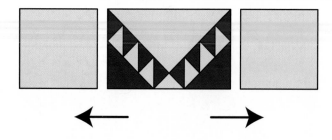

Sew units C on both sides of units AB. Make 2.

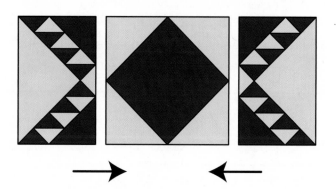

Sew units AB on each side of unit D.

Sew units together as shown.

PIONEER QUILTERS

With busy fingers but with voices gay,
They quilted treasure troves for you and me.
No time for idle thoughts, then, thrifty souls,
Their quilts would live in pictured history.

– Irene F. Cohen

See patterns on pages 64 and 65.

THE TWINKLING STAR

BLOCK SIZE: 12" Finished

Cutting Instructions:

NOTE: *Some strips may have fabric left over. Measurements were figured on 42" wide fabric.*

From the light fabric, cut:

1 – 5 ¼" square.

1 – 4 ½" x 18" strip. Cut the strip into 4 – 4 ½" squares. Cut each square from corner to corner once on the diagonal to make triangles.

1 – 4" x 8" strip. Cut the strip into 2 – 4" squares. Cut each square from corner to corner once on the diagonal to make triangles.

1 – 3 ¼" x 13" strip. Cut the strip into 4 – 3 ¼" squares.

2 – 2 ¼" strips. Cut the strips into 28 – 2 ¼" squares. Cut each square from corner to corner once on the diagonal to make triangles.

From the dark fabric, cut:

1 – 4 ½" x 9" strip. Cut the strip into 2 – 4 ½" squares. Cut each square from corner to corner once on the diagonal to make triangles.

2 – 2 ¼" strips. Cut the strips into 32 – 2 ¼" squares. Cut each square from corner to corner once on the diagonal to make triangles.

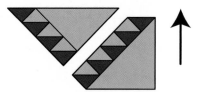

Sew units A to units B.

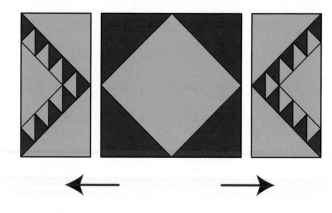

Sew units C to units AB.

Sew units ABC to each side of unit H.

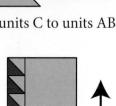

Sew units D to units F.

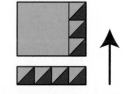

Sew units E to units G.

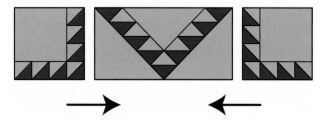

Sew units DF and units EG to each side of units ABC.
Make 2.

Sew the units together as shown.

	Fabric	Position	Size	
Unit A – Make 4				
	Dark	1,3,5,7	2 ¼" x 2 ¼"	◺
	Light	2,4,6	2 ¼" x 2 ¼"	◺
	Light	8	4" x 4"	◺
Unit B – Make 4				
	Dark	1,3,5,7,9	2 ¼" x 2 ¼"	◺
	Light	2,4,6,8	2 ¼" x 2 ¼"	◺
	Light	10	4 ½" x 4 ½"	◺
Unit C – Make 4				
	Light	1	4 ½" x 4 ½"	◺
Units D & E– Make 2 each				
	Light	1,3,5,7	2 ¼" x 2 ¼"	◺
	Dark	2,4,6,8	2 ¼" x 2 ¼"	◺
Units F & G – Make 2 each				
	Light	1,3,5	2 ¼" x 2 ¼"	◺
	Dark	2,4,6	2 ¼" x 2 ¼"	◺
	Light	7	3 ¼" x 3 ¼"	
Unit H – Make 1				
	Light	1	5 ¼" x 5 ¼"	
	Dark	2,3,4,5	4 ½" x 4 ½"	◺

Grannie sits in her oaken chair
The firelight flits o'er her silvery hair,
The silent children around her sit,
As she pieces her patchwork coverlet;
She tells them her story of London Town,
And shows them the scraps of her bridal gown;
Each fragment there is a printed page,
With mem'ries written 'twixt youth and age.

– From the old song, "Patchwork"

See patterns on pages 66 and 67.

FEATHERED EDGE STAR

BLOCK SIZE: 12" Finished

Cutting Instructions:

NOTE: *Some strips may have fabric left over. Measurements were figured on 42" wide fabric.*

From the light fabric, cut:

1 – 5 ¾" x 11 ½" strip. Cut the strip into 2 – 5 ¾" squares. Cut each square from corner to corner once on the diagonal to make triangles.

1 – 4" x 16" strip. Cut the strip into 4 – 4" squares.

2 – 2 ¼" strips. Cut the strips into 28 – 2 ¼" squares. Cut each square from corner to corner once on the diagonal to make triangles.

From the dark fabric, cut:

1 – 3 ½" x 7" strip. Cut the strip into 2 – 3 ½" squares. Cut each square from corner to corner once on the diagonal to make triangles.

1 – 3" x 12" strip. Cut the strip into 4 – 3" squares. Cut each square from corner to corner once on the diagonal to make triangles.

1 – 2 ¾" x 11" strip. Cut the strip into 4 – 2 ¾" squares.

From the solid black fabric, cut:

1 – 3 ½" x 17 ½" strip. Cut the strip into 5 – 3 ½" squares. Cut 4 of the squares from corner to corner once on the diagonal to make 8 triangles.

2 – 2 ¼" strip. Cut the strips into 24 – 2 ¼" squares. Cut each square from corner to corner once on the diagonal to make triangles.

1 – 1 ¾" x 24" strip. Cut the strip into 8 – 1 ¾" x 3" rectangles.

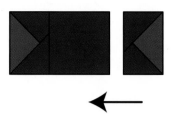

Sew unit A to unit B.

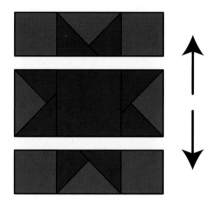

Sew units C on the top and bottom of unit AB.

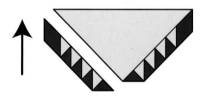

Sew units D to units E.

Sew units F to units DE.

Sew units G to units DEF.

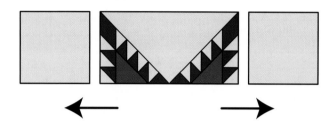

Sew units H to both sides of units DEFG. Make 2.

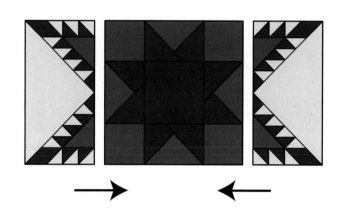

Sew units DEFG to both sides of center unit.

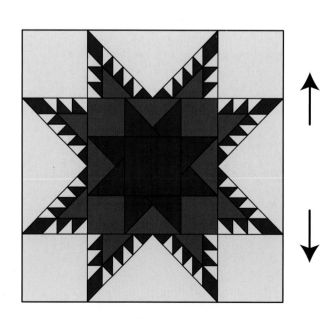

Sew together as shown.

	Fabric	Position	Size	
Unit A – Make 1				
	Dark	1	3 ½" x 3 ½"	◹
	Solid Black	2,3	3 ½" x 3 ½"	◹
	Solid Black	4	3 ½" x 3 ½"	
Unit B – Make 1				
	Dark	1	3 ½" x 3 ½"	◹
	Solid Black	2,3	3 ½" x 3 ½"	◹
Unit C – Make 2				
	Dark	1	3 ½" x 3 ½"	◹
	Solid Black	2,3	3 ½" x 3 ½"	◹
	Dark	4,5	2 ¾" x 2 ¾"	
Unit D – Make 4				
	Solid Black	1	1 ¾" x 3"	
	Light	2,4,6,8	2 ¼" x 2 ¼"	◹
	Solid Black	3,5,7,9	2 ¼" x 2 ¼"	◹
	Light	10	5 ¾" x 5 ¾"	◹
Unit E – Make 4				
	Solid Black	1	1 ¾" x 3 "	
	Light	2,4,6,8	2 ¼" x 2 ¼"	◹
	Solid Black	3,5,7,9	2 ¼" x 2 ¼"	◹
Units F & G – Make 4 each				
	Light	1,3,5	2 ¼" x 2 ¼"	◹
	Solid Black	2,4	2 ¼" x 2 ¼"	◹
	Dark	6	3" x 3"	◹
Unit H – Make 4				
	Light	1	4" x 4"	

GRANDMA'S QUILT

With gentle and loving fingers
She caressed the well worn fold;
'Round each piece a mem'ry lingers
Like a sweet story often told.

– Sylvia Summers Pierce

See patterns on pages 68 and 69.

BLOCK SIZE: 12" Finished

Cutting Instructions:

NOTE: *Some strips may have fabric left over. Measurements were figured on 42" wide fabric.*

From the light fabric, cut:

1 – 5" x 20" strip. Cut the strip into 4 – 5" squares.

1 – 4 ¾" x 9 ½" strip. Cut the strip into 2 – 4 ¾" squares. Cut each square from corner to corner once on the diagonal to make triangles.

1 – 3 ½" x 14" strip. Cut the strip into 4 – 3 ½" squares. Cut each square from corner to corner once on the diagonal to make triangles.

2 – 2 ¼" x 36" strips. Cut the strips into 32 – 2 ¼" squares. Cut each square from corner to corner once on the diagonal to make triangles.

1 – 1 ¾" x 12 ½" strip. Cut the strip into 2 –1 ¾" x 4 ½" rectangles and 2 – 1 ¾" squares.

From the dark fabric, cut:

1 – 3 ½" x 7" strip. Cut the strip into 2 – 3 ½" squares. Cut each square from corner to corner once on the diagonal to make triangles.

2 – 2 ¼" strips. Cut the strips into 20 – 2 ¼" squares. Cut each square from corner to corner once on the diagonal to make triangles.

1 – 2" x 8"strip. Cut the strip into 4 – 2" squares.

1 – 1 ¾" strip. Cut the strip into 8 – 1 ¾" x 2 ¾" rectangles and 9 – 1 ¾" squares.

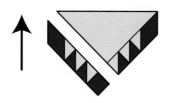

Sew units A to units B.

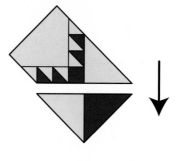

Sew units I to units GH.

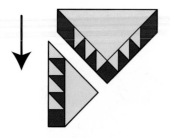

Sew units C to units AB.

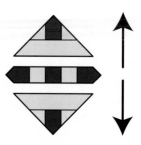

Sew units J to each side of unit K.

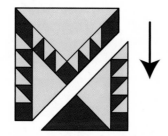

Sew units D to units ABC.

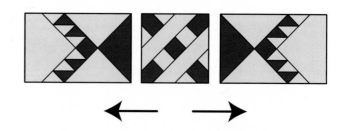

Sew units GJI to each side of unit JK.

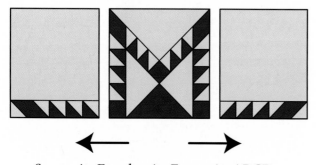

Sew units E and units F to units ABCD.

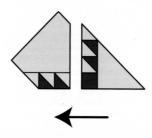

Sew units G to units H.

Sew units together as shown.

	Fabric	Position	Size	
Unit A – Make 2				
	Dark	1	1 ¾" x 2 ¾"	
	Light	2,4,6	2 ¼" x 2 ¼"	◺
	Dark	3,5	2 ¼" x 2 ¼"	◺
	Light	7	4 ¾" x 4 ¾"	◺
Unit B – Make 2				
	Dark	1	1 ¾" x 2 ¾"	
	Light	2,4,6	2 ¼" x 2 ¼"	◺
	Dark	3,5	2 ¼" x 2 ¼"	◺
	Dark	7	1 ¾" x 1 ¾"	
Unit C – Make 2				
	Dark	1	1 ¾" x 1 ¾"	
	Light	2,4,6,8	2 ¼" x 2 ¼"	◺
	Dark	3,5,7	2 ¼" x 2 ¼"	◺
	Light	9	3 ½" x 3 ½"	◺
Unit D – Make 2				
	Dark	1	1 ¾" x 1 ¾"	
	Light	2,4,6,8	2 ¼" x 2 ¼"	◺
	Dark	3,5,7	2 ¼" x 2 ¼"	◺
	Light	9	3 ½" x 3 ½"	◺
	Dark	10	3 ½" x 3 ½"	◺
Units E & F – Make 2 each				
	Dark	1	1 ¾" x 2 ¾"	
	Light	2,3,5,7,9	2 ¼" x 2 ¼"	◺
	Dark	4,6,8	2 ¼" x 2 ¼"	◺
	Light	10	5" x 5"	
Unit G – Make 2				
	Light	1,3,5	2 ¼" x 2 ¼"	◺
	Dark	2,4	2 ¼" x 2 ¼"	◺
	Light	6	4 ¾" x 4 ¾"	◺
Unit H – Make 2				
	Dark	1	1 ¾" x 1 ¾"	
	Light	2,4,6	2 ¼" x 2 ¼"	◺
	Dark	3,5	2 ¼" x 2 ¼"	◺
	Light	7	3 ½" x 3 ½"	◺
Unit I – Make 2				
	Dark	1	3 ½" x 3 ½"	◺
	Light	2	3 ½" x 3 ½"	◺
Unit J – Make 2				
	Dark	1	2" x 2"	
	Light	2,3	2 ¼" x 2 ¼"	◺
	Light	4	1 ¾" x 4 ½"	
Unit K – Make 1				
	Dark	1	1 ¾" x 1 ¾"	
	Light	2,3	1 ¾" x 1 ¾"	
	Dark	4,5	2" x 2"	

See patterns on pages 70 and 71.

Cutting Instructions:

NOTE: *Some strips may have fabric left over. Measurements were figured on 42" wide fabric.*

From the light fabric, cut:

1 – 6" x 12" strip. Cut the strip into 2 – 6" squares. Cut each square from corner to corner once on the diagonal to make triangles.

1 – 4" x 16" strip. Cut the strip into 4 – 4" squares.

1 – 2 ¾" x 5 ½" strip. Cut the strip into 2 – 2 ¾" squares. Cut each square from corner to corner once on the diagonal to make triangles.

2 – 2 ¼" strips. Cut the strips into 26 – 2 ¼" squares. Cut each square from corner to corner once on the diagonal to make triangles.

1 – 1 ¾" x 10"strip. Cut the strip into 4 – 1 ¾" x 2 ½" rectangles.

From the dark fabric, cut:

1 – 5 ¾" square.

1 – 3 ¼" x 13" strip. Cut the strip into 4 – 3 ¼" squares. Cut each square from corner to corner once on the diagonal to make triangles.

2 – 2 ¼" strips. Cut the strips into 22 – 2 ¼" squares. Cut each square from corner to corner once on the diagonal to make triangles.

1 – 2" x 8" strip. Cut the strip into 4 – 2" squares.

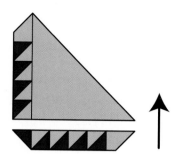

Sew units A to units B.

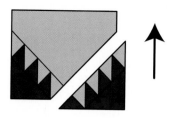

Sew units G to units H.

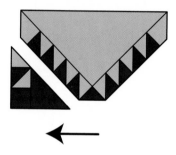

Sew units C to units AB.

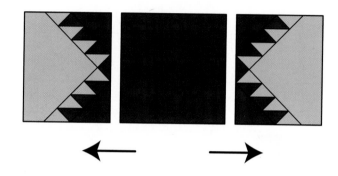

Sew units GH to both side of unit I.

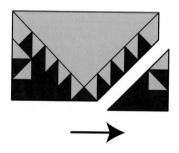

Sew units D to units ABC.

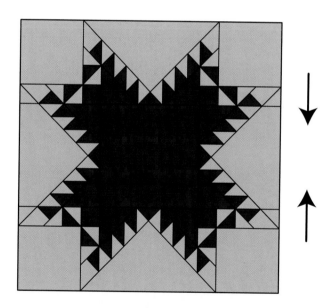

Sew the units together as shown.

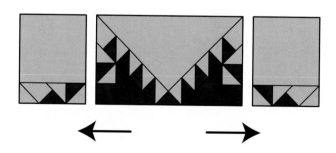

Sew units E and units F to units ABCD.

	Fabric	Position	Size	
Unit A – Make 2				
	Light	1	1 ¾" x 2 ½"	
	Dark	2,4,6,8	2 ¼" x 2 ¼"	◺
	Light	3,5,7,9	2 ¼" x 2 ¼"	◺
	Light	10	6" x 6"	◺
Unit B – Make 2				
	Light	1	1 ¾" x 2 ½"	
	Dark	2,4,6,8,10	2 ¼" x 2 ¼"	◺
	Light	3,5,7,9	2 ¼" x 2 ¼"	◺
Units C & D – Make 2 each				
	Dark	1	2" x 2"	
	Light	2,4	2 ¼" x 2 ¼"	◺
	Dark	3	2 ¼" x 2 ¼"	◺
	Dark	5	3 ¼" x 3 ¼"	◺
Units E & F – Make 2 each				
	Light	1	2 ¾" x 2 ¾"	◺
	Light	2,4,6	2 ¼" x 2 ¼"	◺
	Dark	3,5	2 ¼" x 2 ¼"	◺
	Light	7	4" x 4"	
Unit G – Make 2				
	Light	1,3,5,7	2 ¼" x 2 ¼"	◺
	Dark	2,4,6	2 ¼" x 2 ¼"	◺
	Light	8	6" x 6"	◺
	Dark	9	3 ¼" x 3 ¼"	◺
Unit H – Make 2				
	Dark	1,3,5,7	2 ¼" x 2 ¼"	◺
	Light	2,4,6,8	2 ¼" x 2 ¼"	◺
	Dark	9	3 ¼" x 3 ¼"	◺
Unit I – Make 1				
	Dark	1	5 ¾" x 5 ¾"	

Glad memories are woven unawares
In blending pieces of each favorite dress!
And so this quilt is eloquent today
With happiness that passed not away.

– Amy Smith

See patterns on pages 72 and 73.

STAR-OF-CHAMBLIE

Cutting Instructions:

NOTE: *Some strips may have fabric left over. Measurements were figured on 42" wide fabric.*

From the light fabric, cut:

1 – 5 ½" x 11" strip. Cut the strip into 2 – 5 ½" squares. Cut each square from corner to corner once on the diagonal to make triangles.

1 – 4 ¼ x 17" strip. Cut the strip into 4 – 4 ¼" squares.

1 – 4" square.

2 – 2 ½" strips. Cut the strips into 22 – 2 ½" squares. Cut each square from corner to corner once on the diagonal to make triangles.

From the dark fabric, cut:

1 – 3 ½" x 14" strip. Cut the strip into 4 – 3 ½" squares. Cut each square from corner to corner once on the diagonal to make triangles.

1 – 2 ½" x 30" strip. Cut the strip into 12 – 2 ½" squares. Cut each square from corner to corner once on the diagonal to make triangles.

2 – 2" strips. Cut the strips into 8 – 2" x 3 ½" rectangles and 8 – 2" squares.

1 – 1 ½" x 17 ½" strip. Cut the strip into 2 – 1 ½" x 4 ¾" rectangles and 2 – 1 ½" x 4" rectangles.

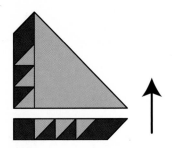

Sew units A to units B.

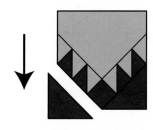

Sew units I to units GH.

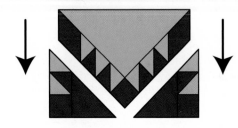

Sew units C and D to each side of unit AB.

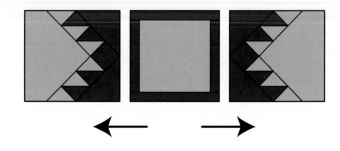

Sew units GHI to each side of unit J.

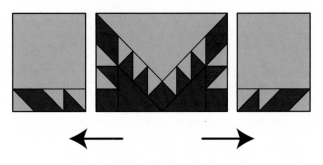

Sew units E and units F to each side of units ABCD.

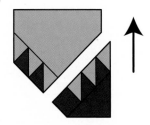

Sew units G to units H.

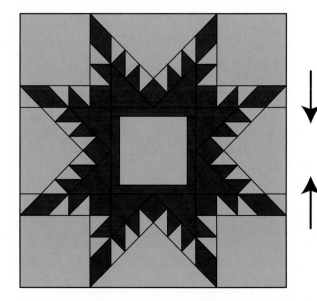

Sew units together as shown.

	Fabric	Position	Size	
Unit A – Make 2				
	Dark	1	2" x 3 ½"	
	Light	2,4,6	2 ½" x 2 ½"	◹
	Dark	3,5	2 ½" x 2 ½"	◹
	Light	7	5 ½" x 5 ½"	◹
Unit B – Make 2				
	Dark	1	2" x 3 ½"	
	Light	2,4,6	2 ½" x 2 ½"	◹
	Dark	3,5	2 ½" x 2 ½"	◹
	Dark	7	2" x 2"	
Units C & D – Make 2 each				
	Dark	1	2" x 2"	
	Light	2,4	2 ½" x 2 ½"	◹
	Dark	3	2 ½" x 2 ½"	◹
	Dark	5	3 ½" x 3 ½"	◹
Units E & F – Make 2 each				
	Dark	1	2" x 3 ½"	
	Light	2,3,5	2 ½" x 2 ½"	◹
	Dark	4	2 ½" x 2 ½"	◹
	Light	6	4 ¼" x 4 ¼"	
Unit G – Make 2				
	Light	1,3,5	2 ½" x 2 ½"	◹
	Dark	2,4	2 ½" x 2 ½"	◹
	Light	6	5 ½" x 5 ½"	◹
Unit H – Make 2				
	Dark	1	2" x 2"	
	Light	2,4,6	2 ½" x 2 ½"	◹
	Dark	3,5	2 ½" x 2 ½"	◹
	Dark	7	3 ½" x 3 ½"	◹
Unit I – Make 2				
	Dark	1	3 ½" x 3 ½"	◹
Unit J – Make 1				
	Light	1	4" x 4"	
	Dark	2,3	1 ½" x 4"	
	Dark	4,5	1 ½" x 4 ¾"	

See patterns on pages 74 and 75.

AUNT BETTY'S STAR

BLOCK SIZE: 12" Finished

Cutting Instructions:

NOTE: *Some strips may have fabric left over. Measurements were figured on 42" wide fabric.*

From the light fabric, cut:

1 – 2 ¼" strip. Cut the strips into 18 – 2 ¼" squares. Cut each square from corner to corner once on the diagonal to make triangles.

1 – 1 ¾" strip. Cut the strip into 8 – 1 ¾" x 3" rectangles and 8 – 1 ¾" squares.

From the dark fabric, cut:

1 – 5" x 10" strip. Cut the strip into 2 – 5" squares. Cut each square from corner to corner once on the diagonal to make triangles.

1 – 4 ½" x 22 ½" strip. Cut the strip into 5 – 4 ½" squares.

1 – 2 ¾" x 28" strip. Cut the strip into 8 – 2 ¾" x 3 ½" rectangles.

1 – 2 ¼" x 4 ½" strip. Cut the strip into 2 – 2 ¼" squares. Cut each square from corner to corner once on the diagonal to make triangles.

From the solid black fabric, cut:

1 – 2 ¾" x 5 ½" strip. Cut the strip into 2 – 2 ¾" squares. Cut the squares from corner to corner once on the diagonal to make triangles.

2 – 2 ¼" strips across the width of fabric. Cut the strips into 24 – 2 ¼" squares. Cut each square from corner to corner once on the diagonal to make triangles.

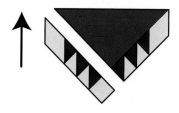

Sew units A to units B.

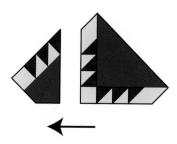

Sew units C to units AB.

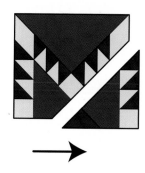

Sew units D to units ABC.

Sew units E and units F to the units ABCD. Make 2.

Sew units G to units H.

Sew units I to units GH.

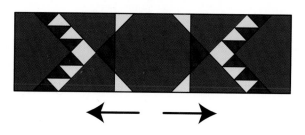

Sew units GHI to each side of unit J.

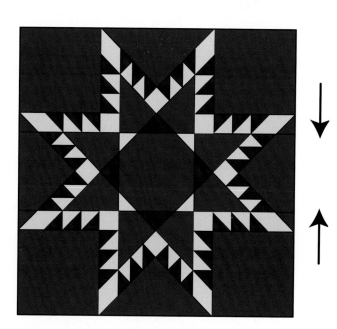

Sew the units together as shown.

	Fabric	Position	Size	
Unit A – Make 2				
	Light	1	1 ¾" x 3"	
	Solid Black	2,4,6	2 ¼" x 2 ¼"	◹
	Light	3,5	2 ¼" x 2 ¼"	◹
	Dark	7	5" x 5"	◹
Unit B – Make 2				
	Light	1	1 ¾" x 3"	
	Solid Black	2,4,6	2 ¼" x 2 ¼"	◹
	Light	3,5	2 ¼" x 2 ¼"	◹
	Light	7	1 ¾" x 1 ¾"	
Units C & H – Make 2 each				
	Light	1	1 ¾" x 1 ¾"	
	Solid Black	2,4,6	2 ¼" x 2 ¼"	◹
	Light	3,5	2 ¼" x 2 ¼"	◹
	Dark	7	2 ¾" x 3 ½"	
Unit D – Make 2 each				
	Light	1	1 ¾" x 1 ¾"	
	Solid Black	2,4,6	2 ¼" x 2 ¼"	◹
	Light	3,5	2 ¼" x 2 ¼"	◹
	Dark	7	2 ¾" x 3 ½"	
	Solid Black	8	2 ¾" x 2 ¾"	◹
Units E & F – Make 2 each				
	Light	1	1 ¾" x 3"	
	Dark	2	2 ¼" x 2 ¼"	◹
	Light	4,6	2 ¼" x 2 ¼"	◹
	Solid Black	3,5,7	2 ¼" x 2 ¼"	◹
	Dark	8	4 ½" x 4 ½"	
Unit G – Make 2				
	Solid Black	1,3,5	2 ¼" x 2 ¼"	◹
	Light	2,4	2 ¼" x 2 ¼"	◹
	Dark	6	5" x 5"	◹
Unit I – Make 2				
	Solid Black	1	2 ¾" x 2 ¾"	◹
	Dark	2	2 ¾" x 3 ½"	
Unit J – Make 1				
	Dark	1	4 ½" x 4 ½"	
	Light	2,3,4,5	2 ¼" x 2 ¼"	◹

See patterns on pages 76 and 77.

BLOCK SIZE: 12" Finished

Cutting Instructions:

NOTE: *Some strips may have fabric left over. Measurements were figured on 42" wide fabric.*

From the light fabric, cut:

1 – 5" x 20" strip. Cut the strip into
4 – 5" squares.

1 – 3 ½" x 16" strip. Cut the strip into
4 – 2 ¼" x 3 ½" rectangles and
4 – 1 ¾" x 3 ½" rectangles.

1 – 3 ¼" x 6 ½" strip. Cut the strip into
2 – 3 ¼" squares. Cut each square from corner to corner once on the diagonal to make triangles.

3 – 2 ¼" strips. Cut the strips into
50 – 2 ¼" squares. Cut each square from corner to corner once on the diagonal to make triangles.

1 – 1 ¾" x 14" strip. Cut the strip into
8 – 1 ¾" squares.

From the dark fabric, cut:

1 – 2 ¾" x 5 ½" strip. Cut the strip into 2 – 2 ¾" squares. Cut each square from corner to corner once on the diagonal to make triangles.

1 – 2 ½" x 34" strip. Cut the strip into 8 – 2 ½" x 4 ¼" rectangles.

3 – 2 ¼" strips. Cut the strips into 44 – 2 ¼" squares. Cut each square from corner to corner once on the diagonal to make triangles.

1 – 1 ¾" x 22 ¾" strip. Cut the strip into 13 – 1 ¾" squares.

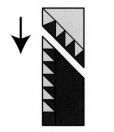 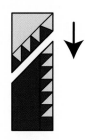

Sew units A to units C and sew units B to units D.

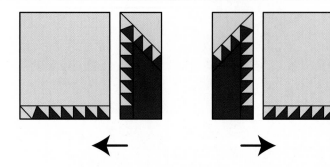

Sew units AC to units E and sew units BD to units F.

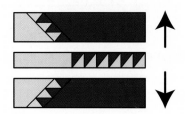

Sew units G and H to both sides of units J.

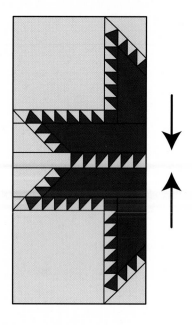

Sew units together as shown.

Sew units to both sides of unit I as shown.

	Fabric	Position	Size	
Units A & B – Make 2 each				
	Light	1	1 ¾" x 1 ¾"	
	Dark	2	1 ¾" x 1 ¾"	
	Light	3,5,7	2 ¼" x 2 ¼"	◺
	Dark	4,6,8	2 ¼" x 2 ¼"	◺
	Light	9	3 ¼" x 3 ¼"	◺
Units C & D – Make 2 each				
	Dark	1	1 ¾" x 1 ¾"	
	Light	2,4,6,8,10,12	2 ¼" x 2 ¼"	◺
	Dark	3,5,7,9,11	2 ¼" x 2 ¼"	◺
	Dark	13	2 ¼" x 4 ¼"	
Units E & F – Make 2 each				
	Light	1	1 ¾" x 1 ¾"	
	Dark	2	1 ¾" x 1 ¾"	
	Light	3,4,6,8,10,12,14	2 ¼" x 2 ¼"	◺
	Dark	5,7,9,11,13	2 ¼" x 2 ¼"	◺
	Light	15	5" x 5"	
Units G & H – Make 2 each				
	Dark	1,3,5	2 ¼" x 2 ¼"	◺
	Light	2,4,6	2 ¼" x 2 ¼"	◺
	Light	7	2 ¼" x 3 ½"	
	Dark	8	2 ¾" x 2 ¾"	◺
	Dark	9	2 ½" x 4 ¼"	
Unit I – Make 1				
	Dark	1	1 ¾" x 1 ¾"	
	Light	2,4,6,8,10,12,14, 16,18,20,22,24	2 ¼" x 2 ¼"	◺
	Dark	3,5,7,9,11,13,15 17,19,21,23,25	2 ¼" x 2 ¼"	◺
	Light	26,27	1 ¾" x 3 ½"	
Unit J – Make 2				
	Light	1	1 ¾" x 3 ½"	
	Dark	2,4,6,8,10,12	2 ¼" x 2 ¼"	◺
	Light	3,5,7,9,11,13	2 ¼" x 2 ¼"	◺

...blossemed the lovely stars, the forget-me-nots of the angels.

– Longfellow's *Evangeline*

See patterns on pages 78 and 79.

FEATHERED STAR NO. 2

Cutting Instructions:

NOTE: *Some strips may have fabric left over. Measurements were figured on 42" wide fabric.*

From the light fabric, cut:

1 – 4 ½" x 18" strip. Cut the strip into 4 – 4 ½" squares.

1 – 3 ¾" x 18" strip. Cut the strip into 4 – 3 ¾" x 4 ½" rectangles.

2 – 2 ½" strips. Cut the strips into 18 – 2 ½" squares. Cut each square from corner to corner once on the diagonal to make triangles.

From the dark fabric, cut:

1 – 4 ¾" x 9 ½" strip. Cut the strip into 2 – 4 ¾" squares. Cut each square from corner to corner once on the diagonal to make triangles.

1 – 4 ½" square.

1 – 4" x 8" strip. Cut the strip into 2 – 4" squares. Cut each square from corner to corner once on the diagonal to make triangles.

2 – 2 ½" strips. Cut the strips into 18 – 2 ½" squares. Cut each square from corner to corner once on the diagonal to make triangles.

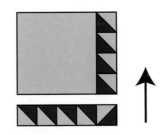

Sew units A to units B.

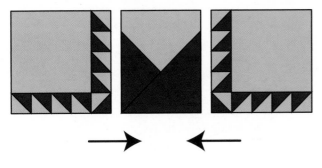

Sew units AB to each side of units C.

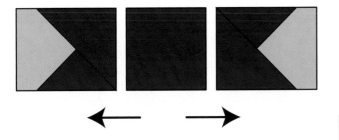

Sew units C to each side of units D.

Sew units together as shown.

	Fabric	Position	Size	
Unit A – Make 4				
	Light	1,3,5,7	2 ½" x 2 ½"	◣
	Dark	2,4,6,8	2 ½" x 2 ½"	◣
	Light	9	4 ½" x 4 ½"	
Unit B – Make 4				
	Dark	1,3,5,7,9	2 ½" x 2 ½"	◣
	Light	2,4,6,8,10	2 ½" x 2 ½"	◣
Unit C – Make 4				
	Light	1	3 ¾" x 4 ½"	
	Dark	2	4" x 4"	◣
	Dark	3	4 ¾" x 4 ¾"	◣
Unit D – Make 1				
	Dark	1	4 ½" x 4 ½"	

See pattern on page 80.

FEATHERED STAR VARIATION

Cutting Instructions:

NOTE: *Some strips may have fabric left over. Measurements were figured on 42" wide fabric.*

From the light fabric, cut:

1 – 5 ¾" x 11 ½" strip. Cut the strip into 2 – 5 ¾" squares. Cut each square from corner to corner once on the diagonal to make triangles.

1 – 4 ½" x 18" strip. Cut the strip into 4 – 4 ½" squares.

1 – 3 ¼" x 6 ½" strip. Cut the strip into 2 – 3 ¼" squares. Cut each square from corner to corner once on the diagonal to make triangles.

1 – 2 ½" x 10" strip. Cut the strip into 4 – 2 ½" squares.

2 – 2 ¼" strips. Cut the strips into 22 – 2 ¼" squares. Cut each square from corner to corner once on the diagonal to make triangles.

From the dark fabric, cut:

1 – 3 ¼" x 13" strip. Cut the strip into 4 – 3 ¼" squares. Cut each square from corner to corner once on the diagonal to make triangles.

2 – 2 ¼" strips. Cut the strips into 28 – 2 ¼" squares. Cut each square from corner to corner once on the diagonal to make triangles.

From the solid black fabric, cut:

1 – 3 ½" square.

1 – 2" x 25" strip. Cut the strip into 4 – 2" x 2 ¾" rectangles and 4 – 2" x 3 ½" rectangles.

1 – 1 ¾" x 24" strip. Cut the strip into 8 – 1 ¾" x 3" rectangles.

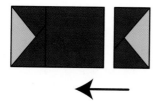

Sew unit A to unit B.

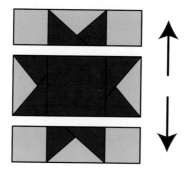

Sew units C on both sides of unit AB.

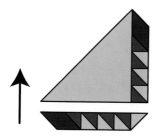

Sew units D to units E.

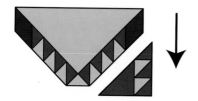

Sew units F to units DE.

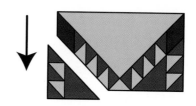

Sew units G to units DEF.

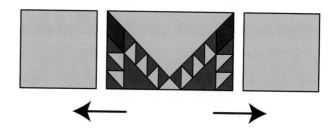

Sew units H to both sides of units DEFG. Make 2.

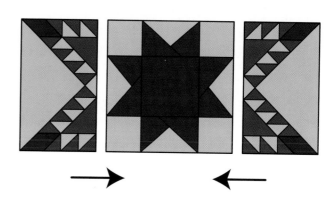

Sew units DEFG to both sides of unit ABC.

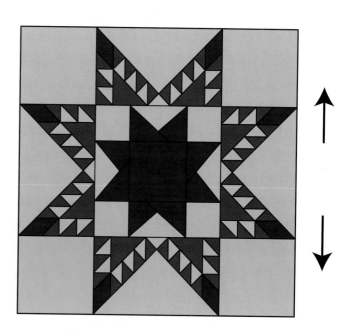

Sew units together as shown.

	Fabric	Position	Size	
Unit A – Make 1				
	Light	1	3 ¼" x 3 ¼"	◺
	Solid Black	2	2" x 2 ¾"	
	Solid Black	3	2" x 3 ½"	
	Solid Black	4	3 ½" x 3 ½"	
Unit B – Make 1				
	Light	1	3 ¼" x 3 ¼"	◺
	Solid Black	2	2" x 2 ¾"	
	Solid Black	3	2" x 3 ½"	
Unit C – Make 2				
	Light	1	3 ¼" x 3 ¼"	◺
	Solid Black	2	2" x 2 ¾"	
	Solid Black	3	2" x 3 ½"	
	Light	4,5	2 ½" x 2 ½"	
Unit D – Make 4				
	Solid Black	1	1 ¾" x 3"	
	Dark	2,4,6,8	2 ¼" x 2 ¼"	◺
	Light	3,5,7	2 ¼" x 2 ¼"	◺
	Light	9	5 ¾" x 5 ¾"	◺
Unit E – Make 4				
	Solid Black	1	1 ¾" x 3"	
	Dark	2,4,6,8	2 ¼" x 2 ¼"	◺
	Light	3,5,7,9	2 ¼" x 2 ¼"	◺
Units F & G – Make 4 each				
	Dark	1,3,5	2 ¼" x 2 ¼"	◺
	Light	2,4	2 ¼" x 2 ¼"	◺
	Dark	6	3 ¼" x 3 ¼"	◺
Unit H – Make 4				
	Light	1	4 ½" x 4 ½"	

Work which grows beautiful under one's own hands is truly a pleasure, and what more so than the making of a patchwork quilt?

– Carrie H. Hall

See patterns on pages 81 and 82.

FEATHERED STAR NO. 3

BLOCK SIZE: 12" Finished

Cutting Instructions:

NOTE: *Some strips may have fabric left over. Measurements were figured on 42" wide fabric.*

From the light fabric, cut:

1 – 5" x 20" strip. Cut the strip into 4 – 5" squares.

1 – 4 ½" x 9" strip. Cut the strip into 2 – 4 ½" squares. Cut each square from corner to corner once on the diagonal to make triangles.

2 – 2 ½" strips. Cut the strips into 28 – 2 ½" squares. Cut each square from corner to corner once on the diagonal to make triangles.

From the dark fabric, cut:

1 – 3 ½" x 14" strip. Cut the strip into 4 – 3 ½" squares. Cut each square from corner to corner once on the diagonal to make triangles.

1 – 3" x 9" strip. Cut the strip into 3 – 3" squares. Cut 2 squares from corner to corner once on the diagonal to make triangles.

2 – 2 ½" strips. Cut the strips into 18 – 2 ½" squares. Cut each square from corner to corner once on the diagonal to make triangles.

1 – 2" x 8" strip. Cut the strip into 4 – 2" squares.

1 – 1 ¾" x 26" strip. Cut the strip into 8 – 1 ¾" x 3 ¼" rectangles.

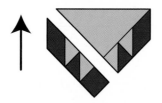

Sew units A to units B.

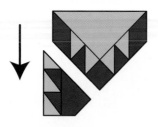

Sew units C to units AB.

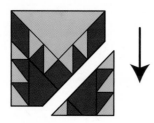

Sew units D to units ABC.

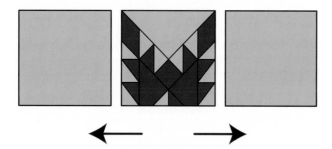

Sew units E to each side of units ABCD. Make 2

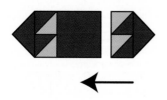

Sew unit F to unit G.

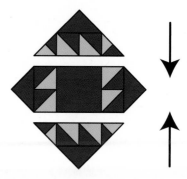

Sew units H to each side of unit FG.

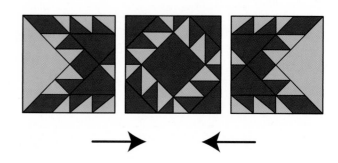

Sew units ABCD to each side of unit FGH.

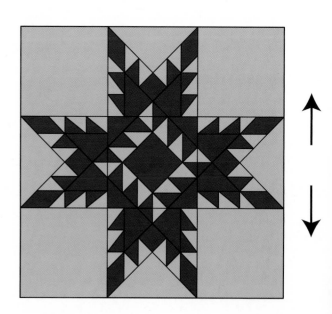

Sew units together as shown.

	Fabric	Position	Size	
Unit A – Make 4				
	Dark	1	1 ¾" x 3 ¼"	
	Light	2,4	2 ½" x 2 ½"	◰
	Dark	3	2 ½" x 2 ½"	◰
	Light	5	4 ½" x 4 ½"	◰
Unit B – Make 4				
	Dark	1	1 ¾" x 3 ¼"	
	Light	2,4	2 ½" x 2 ½"	◰
	Dark	3	2 ½" x 2 ½"	◰
	Dark	5	2" x 2"	
Unit C – Make 4				
	Light	1,3,5	2 ½" x 2 ½"	◰
	Dark	2,4	2 ½" x 2 ½"	◰
	Dark	6	3 ½" x 3 ½"	◰
Unit D – Make 4				
	Light	1,3,5,7	2 ½" x 2 ½"	◰
	Dark	2,4	2 ½" x 2 ½"	◰
	Dark	6	3 ½" x 3 ½"	◰
Unit E – Make 4				
	Light	1	5" x 5"	
Unit F – Make 1				
	Light	1,3	2 ½" x 2 ½"	◰
	Dark	2,4	2 ½" x 2 ½"	◰
	Dark	5	3" x 3"	◰
	Dark	6	3" x 3"	
Unit G – Make 1				
	Dark	1,3	2 ½" x 2 ½"	◰
	Light	2,4	2 ½" x 2 ½"	◰
	Dark	5	3" x 3"	◰
Unit H – Make 2				
	Dark	1,3,5,7	2 ½" x 2 ½"	◰
	Light	2,4,6,8	2 ½" x 2 ½"	◰
	Dark	9	3" x 3"	◰

See pattern on pages 83 and 84.

THE HOUR GLASS

BLOCK SIZE: 12" Finished

Cutting Instructions:

NOTE: *Some strips may have fabric left over. Measurements were figured on 42" wide fabric.*

From the light fabric, cut:

1 – 5 ½" x 24" strip. Cut the strip into 8 – 3" x 5 ½" rectangles.

1 – 4" x 19" strip. Cut the strip into 4 – 4" x 4 ¾" rectangles.

1 – 3 ½" x 14" strip. Cut the strip into 4 – 3 ½" squares.

1 – 2 ¾" x 27 ½" strip. Cut the strip into 10 – 2 ¾" squares. Cut each square from corner to corner once on the diagonal to make triangles.

From the dark fabric, cut:

1 – 5 ¾" square.

1 – 2 ¾" x 27 ½" strip. Cut the strip into 10 – 2 ¾" squares. Cut each square from corner to corner once on the diagonal to make triangles.

2 – 1 ½" x 23" strips. Cut the strips into 4 – 1 ½" x 5" rectangles and 4 – 1 ½" x 5 ¾" rectangles.

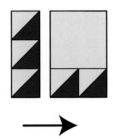

Sew units A to units B.

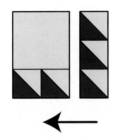

Sew units C to units D.

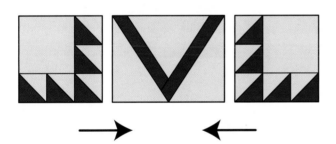

Sew units AB and units CD to units E.

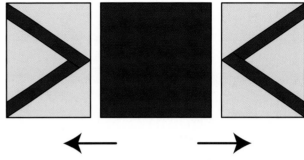

Sew units E to both sides of unit F.

Sew the units together as shown.

See pattern on pages 85 and 86.

	Fabric	Position	Size	
Units A & C – Make 2 each				
	Dark	1,3,5	2 ¾" x 2 ¾"	◺
	Light	2,4,6	2 ¾" x 2 ¾"	◺
Units B & D – Make 2 each				
	Dark	1,3	2 ¾" x 2 ¾"	◺
	Light	2,4	2 ¾" x 2 ¾"	◺
	Light	5	3 ½" x 3 ½	
Unit E – Make 4				
	Light	1	4" x 4 ¾"	
	Dark	2	1 ½" x 5"	
	Dark	3	1 ½" x 5 ¾"	
	Light	4,5	3" x 5 ½"	
Unit F – Make 1				
	Dark	1	5 ¾" x 5 ¾"	

FEATHERED STAR NO. 6

BLOCK SIZE: 12" Finished

Cutting Instructions:

NOTE: *Some strips may have fabric left over. Measurements were figured on 42" wide fabric.*

From the light fabric, cut:

1 – 5 ¼" x 21" strip. Cut the strip into 4 – 5 ¼" squares.

1 – 2 ¾" x 11" strip. Cut the strip into 4 – 2 ¾" squares.

2 – 2 ½" strips. Cut the strips into 22 – 2 ½" squares. Cut each square from corner to corner once on the diagonal to make triangles.

1 – 2 ¼" x 9" strip. Cut the strip into 4 – 2 ¼" squares.

From the dark fabric, cut:

1 – 4 ½" square.

1 – 3 ¼" x 6 ½" strip. Cut the strip into 2 – 3 ¼" squares. Cut each square from corner to corner once on the diagonal to make triangles.

1 – 2 ¾" x 16 ½" strip. Cut the strip into 6 – 2 ¾" squares. Cut each square from corner to corner once on the diagonal to make triangles.

2 – 2 ½" strips. Cut the strips into 20 – 2 ½" squares. Cut each square from corner to corner once on the diagonal to make triangles.

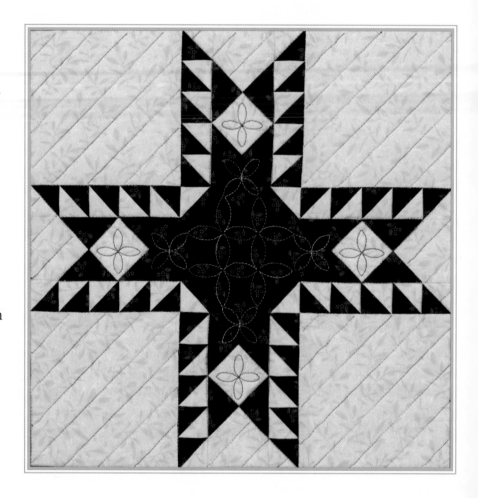

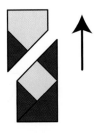

Sew units A to units B.

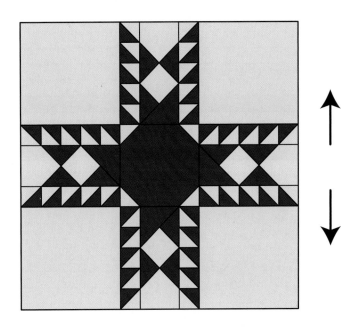

Sew units together as shown.

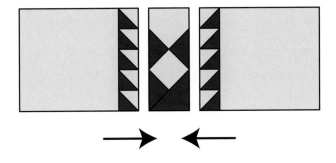

Sew units C and units D to units AB. Make 2.

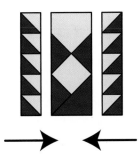

Sew units E and units F to units AB. Make 2.

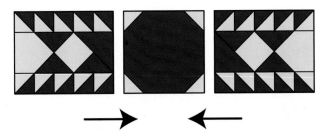

Sew units ABEF to unit G.

	Fabric	Position	Size	
Unit A – Make 4				
	Light	1	2 ¼" x 2 ¼"	
	Dark	2,3	2 ¾" x 2 ¾"	
	Dark	4	3 ¼" x 3 ¼"	
Unit B – Make 4				
	Light	1	2 ¾" x 2 ¾"	
	Dark	2	2 ¾" x 2 ¾"	
Units C & D – Make 2 each				
	Dark	1,3,5,7,9	2 ½" x 2 ½"	
	Light	2,4,6,8,10	2 ½" x 2 ½"	
	Light	11	5 ¼" x 5 ¼"	
Units E & F – Make 2 each				
	Light	1,3,5,7,9	2 ½" x 2 ½"	
	Dark	2,4,6,8,10	2 ½" x 2 ½"	
Unit G – Make 1				
	Dark	1	4 ½" x 4 ½"	
	Light	2,3,4,5	2 ½" x 2 ½"	

Made by Carolyn Cullinan McCormick.
Quilted by Carol Willey, Castle Rock, Colo.

See patterns on pages 87 and 88.

FEATHERED STAR NO. 1

BLOCK SIZE: 12" Finished

Cutting Instructions:

NOTE: *Some strips may have fabric left over. Measurements were figured on 42" wide fabric.*

From the light fabric, cut:

1 – 5 ¾" x 11 ½" strip. Cut the strip into 2 – 5 ¾" squares. Cut each square from corner to corner once on the diagonal to make triangles.

1 – 4" x 20" strip. Cut the strip into 5 – 4" squares.

1 – 3 ½" x 7" strip. Cut the strip into 2 – 3 ½" squares. Cut each square from corner to corner once on the diagonal to make triangles.

2 – 2 ¼" strips. Cut the strips into 34 – 2 ¼" squares. Cut each square from corner to corner once on the diagonal to make triangles.

1 – 1 ½" x 6" strip. Cut the strip into 4 – 1 ½" squares.

From the dark fabric, cut:

1 – 3 ½" x 14" strip. Cut the strip into 4 – 3 ½" squares. Cut each square from corner to corner once on the diagonal to make triangles.

2 – 2 ¼" strips. Cut the strips into 26 – 2 ¼" squares. Cut each square from corner to corner once on the diagonal to make triangles.

1 – 1 ¾" strip. Cut the strip into 4 – 1 ¾" x 4" rectangles and 8 – 1 ¾" x 2 ¾" rectangles.

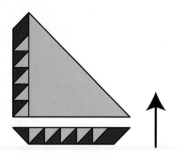

Sew units A to units B.

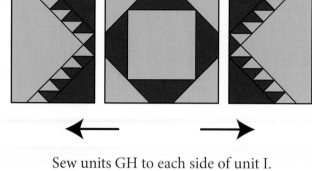

Sew units GH to each side of unit I.

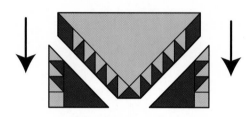

Sew units C and units D to each side of units AB.

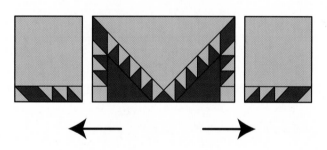

Sew units E and units F to each side of units ABCD.

Sew the units together as shown.

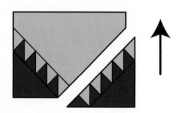

Sew units G to units H.

	Fabric	Position	Size	
Unit A – Make 2				
	Dark	1	1 ¾" x 2 ¾"	
	Light	2,4,6,8,10	2 ¼" x 2 ¼"	◳
	Dark	3,5,7,9	2 ¼" x 2 ¼"	◳
	Light	11	5 ¾" x 5 ¾"	◳
Unit B – Make 2				
	Dark	1	1 ¾" x 2 ¾"	
	Light	2,4,6,8,10	2 ¼" x 2 ¼"	◳
	Dark	3,5,7,9,11	2 ¼" x 2 ¼"	◳
Units C & D – Make 2 each				
	Light	1	1 ½" x 1 ½"	
	Light	2,4,6	2 ¼" x 2 ¼"	◳
	Dark	3,5	2 ¼" x 2 ¼"	◳
	Dark	7	3 ½" x 3 ½"	◳
Units E & F – Make 2 each				
	Dark	1	1 ¾" x 2 ¾"	
	Light	2,3,5,7	2 ¼" x 2 ¼"	◳
	Dark	4,6	2 ¼" x 2 ¼"	◳
	Light	8	4" x 4"	
Unit G – Make 2				
	Light	1,3,5,7,9	2 ¼" x 2 ¼"	◳
	Dark	2,4,6,8	2 ¼" x 2 ¼"	◳
	Dark	10	3 ½" x 3 ½"	◳
	Light	11	5 ¾" x 5 ¾"	◳
Unit H – Make 2				
	Dark	1,3,5,7,9	2 ¼" x 2 ¼"	◳
	Light	2,4,6,8,10	2 ¼" x 2 ¼"	◳
	Dark	11	3 ½" x 3 ½"	◳
Unit I – Make 1				
	Light	1	4" x 4"	
	Dark	2,3,4,5	1 ¾" x 4"	
	Light	6,7,8,9	3 ½ x 3 ½"	◳

The sun has such a pretty quilt
Each night he goes to bed,
It's made of lavender and gold,
With great long stripes of red.

And bordered by the softest tints
Of all the shades of gray.
It's put together by the sky,
And quilted by the day.

– Laura Coates Reed

See patterns on pages 89 and 90.

FEATHERED STAR, FINLEY

BLOCK SIZE: 12" Finished

Cutting Instructions:

NOTE: *Some strips may have fabric left over. Measurements were figured on 42" wide fabric.*

From the light fabric, cut:

1 – 5 ¾" x 11 ½" strip. Cut the strip into 2 – 5 ¾" squares. Cut each square from corner to corner once on the diagonal to make triangles.

1 – 4 ¼" x 17" strip. Cut the strip into 4 – 4 ¼" squares.

1 – 2 ¼" x 31 ½" strip. Cut the strip into 14 – 2 ¼" squares. Cut each square from corner to corner once on the diagonal to make triangles.

1 – 2" strip. Cut the strip into 20 – 2" squares. Cut each square from corner to corner once on the diagonal to make triangles.

From the dark fabric, cut:

1 – 5 ½" square.

1 – 3 ¾" x 15" strip. Cut the strip into 4 – 3 ¾" squares. Cut each square from corner to corner once on the diagonal to make triangles.

1 – 2 ¼" x 18" strip. Cut the strip into 8 – 2 ¼" squares. Cut each square from corner to corner once on the diagonal to make triangles.

1 – 2" x 32" strip. Cut the strip into 16 – 2" squares. Cut each square from corner to corner once on the diagonal to make triangles.

1 – 1 ¾" x 36" strip. Cut the strip into 8 – 1 ¾" squares and 8 – 1 ¾" x 2 ¾" rectangles.

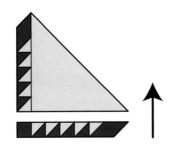

Sew units A to units B.

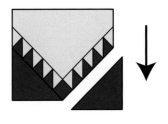

Sew units I to unit GH.

Sew units C and units D to units AB.

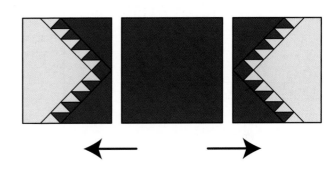

Sew units GHI to both sides of unit J.

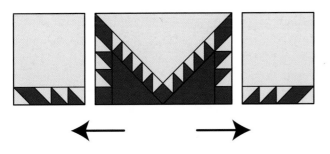

Sew units E and units F to units ABC.

Sew the units together as shown.

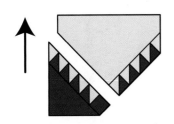

Sew units G to units H.

	Fabric	Position	Size	
Unit A – Make 2				
	Dark	1	1 ¾" x 2 ¾"	
	Light	2,4,6,8,10	2" x 2"	◩
	Dark	3,5,7,9	2" x 2"	◩
	Light	11	5 ¾" x 5 ¾"	◩
Unit B – Make 2				
	Dark	1	1 ¾" x 2 ¾"	
	Light	2,4,6,8,10	2" x 2"	◩
	Dark	3,5,7,9	2" x 2"	◩
	Dark	11	1 ¾" x 1 ¾"	
Units C & D – Make 2 each				
	Dark	1	1 ¾" x 1 ¾"	
	Light	2,4,6	2 ¼" x 2 ¼"	◩
	Dark	3,5	2 ¼" x 2 ¼"	◩
	Dark	7	3 ¾" x 3 ¾"	◩
Units E & F – Make 2 each				
	Dark	1	1 ¾" x 2 ¾"	
	Light	2,4,6,7	2 ¼" x 2 ¼"	◩
	Dark	3,5	2 ¼" x 2 ¼"	◩
	Light	8	4 ¼" x 4 ¼"	
Unit G – Make 2				
	Dark	1	1 ¾" x 1 ¾"	
	Light	2,4,6,8,10	2" x 2"	◩
	Dark	3,5,7,9	2" x 2"	◩
	Dark	11	3 ¾" x 3 ¾"	◩
Unit H – Make 2				
	Light	1,3,5,7,9	2" x 2"	◩
	Dark	2,4,6,8	2" x 2"	◩
	Light	10	5 ¾" x 5 ¾"	◩
Unit I – Make 2				
	Dark	1	3 ¾" x 3 ¾"	◩
Unit J – Make 1				
	Dark	1	5 ½" x 5 ½"	

Curiously wrought in stitches, line on line,
Faded, yet fair, these ancient calicoes
Bespeak the patient work of one who knows
No weariness in finish or design.
        – Amy Smith

See patterns on pages 91 and 92.

CHESTNUT BURR

BLOCK SIZE: 12" Finished

Cutting Instructions:

NOTE: *Some strips may have fabric left over. Measurements were figured on 42" wide fabric.*

From the light fabric, cut:

1 – 6" x 12" strip. Cut the strip into 2 – 6" squares. Cut the square from corner to corner once on the diagonal to make triangles.

1 – 4" x 16" strip. Cut the strip into 4 – 4" squares.

1 – 3 ¼" x 13" strip. Cut the strip into 4 – 3 ¼" squares. Cut each square from corner to corner once on the diagonal to make triangles.

2 – 2 ¼" strips. Cut the strips into 26 – 2 ¼" squares. Cut each square from corner to corner once on the diagonal to make triangles.

1 – 1 ¾" x 18" strip. Cut the strips into 8 – 1 ¾" x 2 ¼" rectangles.

From the dark fabric, cut:

1 – 5 ¾" square.

2 – 2 ¼" strips. Cut the strips into 22 – 2 ¼" squares. Cut each square from corner to corner once on the diagonal to make triangles.

1 – 1 ¾" x 7" strip. Cut the strip into 4 – 1 ¾" squares.

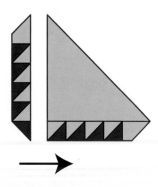

Sew units A to units B.

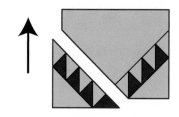

Sew units G to units H.

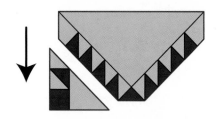

Sew units C to units AB.

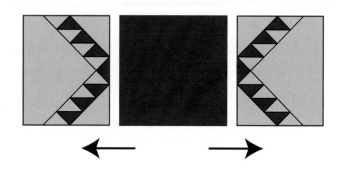

Sew units GH to both sides of unit I.

Sew units D to units ABC.

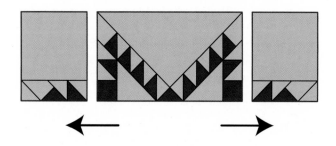

Sew units E and units F to units ABCD. Make 2

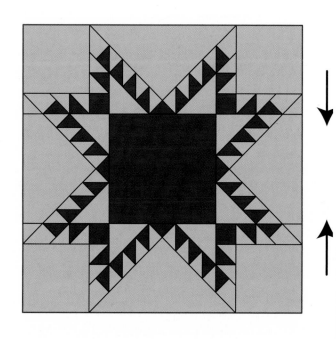

Sew units together as shown.

	Fabric	Position	Size	
Unit A – Make 2				
	Light	1	1 ¾" x 2 ¼"	
	Dark	2,4,6,8	2 ¼" x 2 ¼"	◳
	Light	3,5,7,9	2 ¼" x 2 ¼"	◳
	Light	10	6" x 6"	◳
Unit B – Make 2				
	Light	1	1 ¾" x 2 ¼"	
	Dark	2,4,6,8,10	2 ¼" x 2 ¼"	◳
	Light	3,5,7,9	2 ¼" x 2 ¼"	◳
Units C & D – Make 2 each				
	Dark	1	1 ¾" x 1 ¾"	
	Light	2,4	2 ¼" x 2 ¼"	◳
	Dark	3	2 ¼" x 2 ¼"	◳
	Light	5	3 ¼" x 3 ¼"	◳
Units E & F – Make 2 each				
	Light	1	1 ¾" x 2 ¼"	
	Light	2,4,6	2 ¼" x 2 ¼"	◳
	Dark	3,5	2 ¼" x 2 ¼"	◳
	Light	7	4" x 4"	
Unit G – Make 2				
	Light	1,3,5,7	2 ¼" x 2 ¼"	◳
	Dark	2,4,6	2 ¼" x 2 ¼"	◳
	Light	8	3 ¼" x 3 ¼"	◳
	Light	9	6" x 6"	◳
Unit H – Make 2				
	Dark	1,3,5,7	2 ¼" x 2 ¼"	◳
	Light	2,4,6,8	2 ¼" x 2 ¼"	◳
	Light	9	3 ¼" x 3 ¼"	◳
Unit I – Make 1				
	Dark	1	5 ¾" x 5 ¾"	

EACH STITCH

The stitches in this quilt-patch rare,
Were patiently made with loving care;
If each thought put forth were as perfect and true,
It would make a grand world for me and you.

– Ida H. Frederick

See patterns on pages 93 and 94.

CALIFORNIA STAR

BLOCK SIZE: 24" Finished

Cutting Instructions:

NOTE: *Some strips may have fabric left over. Measurements were figured on 42" wide fabric.*

From the light fabric, cut:

1 – 9 ½" x 19" strip. Cut the strip into
2 – 9 ½" squares. Cut each square from corner to corner once on the diagonal to make triangles

1 – 7 ½" x 30" strip. Cut the strip into
4 – 7 ½" squares.

3 – 2 ¾" strips. Cut the strips into
36 – 2 ¾" squares. Cut each square from corner to corner once on the diagonal to make triangles

2 – 2 ½" strips. Cut the strips into
20 – 2 ½" squares. Cut each square from corner to corner once on the diagonal to make triangles.

2 – 2 ¼" strips. Cut the strips into 20 – 2 ¼" squares.

From the dark fabric, cut:

1 – 5 ¼" x 21" strip. Cut the strip into 4 – 5 ¼" squares. Cut each square from corner to corner once on the diagonal to make triangles.

1 – 4 ¾" x 19" strip. Cut the strip into 4 – 4 ¾" squares.

2 – 2 ¾" strips. Cut the strips into 30 – 2 ¾" squares. Cut each square from corner to corner once on the diagonal to make triangles.

2 – 2 ½" strips. Cut the strips into 20 – 2 ½" squares. Cut each square from corner to corner once on the diagonal to make triangles.

2 – 2 ¼" strips. Cut the strips into 8 – 2 ¼" x 4" rectangles and 5 – 2 ¼" squares.

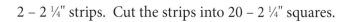

Sew units B and units C on both sides of units A. Make 5.

Sew units D and E together. Make 10.

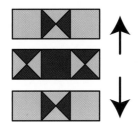

Sew units DE on top and bottom of units ABC. Make 5.

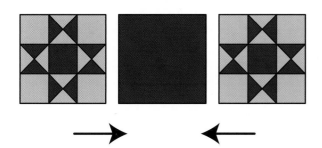

Sew units ABC to both sides of units F. Make 2.

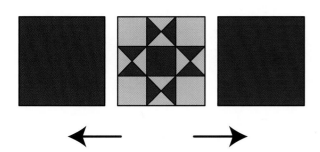

Sew units F to both sides of unit ABC. Make 1.

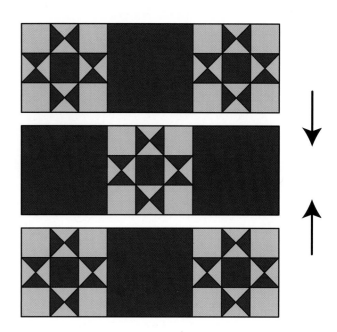

Sew the units together as shown.

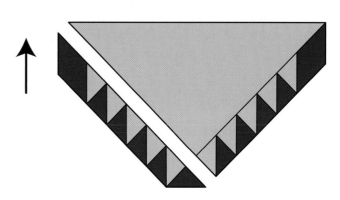

Sew units G to units H.

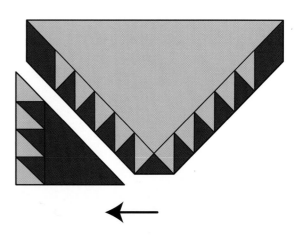

Sew units I to units GH.

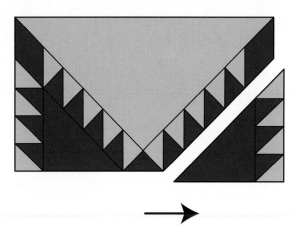

Sew units J to units GHI.

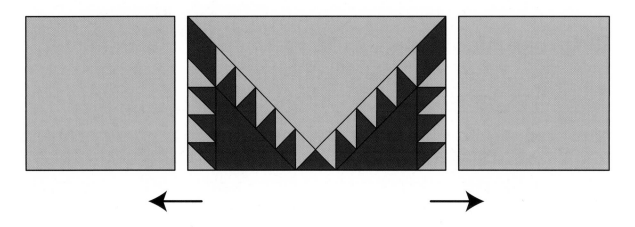

Sew units K to units GHIJ. Make 2.

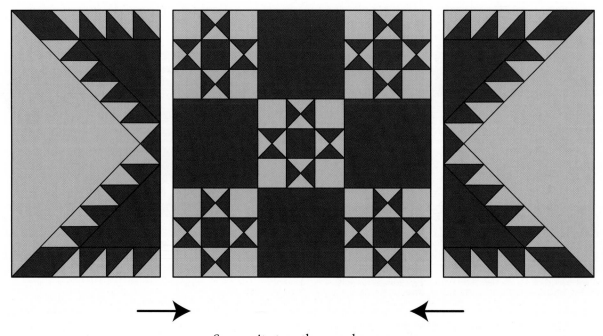

Sew units together as shown.

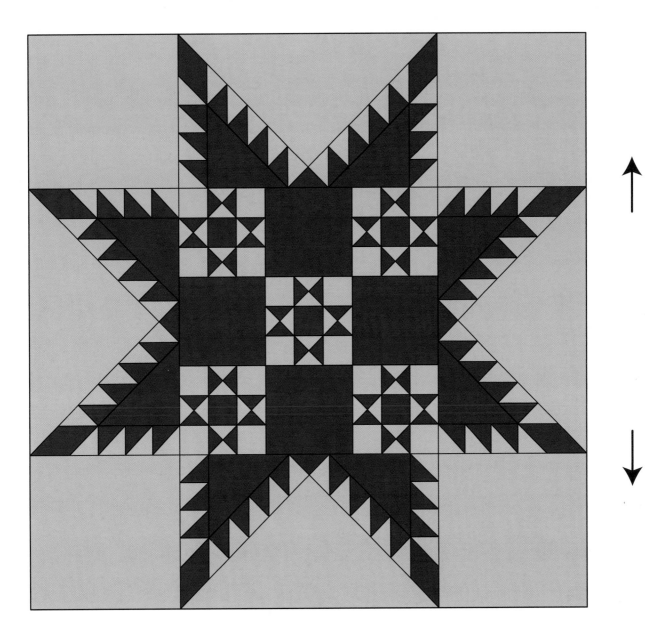

Sew units together as shown.

Made and quilted by
Carolyn Cullinan McCormick

	Fabric	Position	Size	
Unit A – Make 5				
	Dark	1	2 ¼" x 2 ¼"	
	Light	2,3	2 ½" x 2 ½"	◻
	Dark	4,5	2 ½" x 2 ½"	◻
Units B & C– Make 5 each				
	Light	1	2 ½" x 2 ½"	◻
	Dark	2	2 ½" x 2 ½"	◻
Units D & E – Make 10 each				
	Light	1	2 ½" x 2 ½"	◻
	Dark	2	2 ½" x 2 ½"	◻
	Light	3	2 ¼" x 2 ¼"	
Unit F – Make 4				
	Dark	1	4 ¾" x 4 ¾"	
Unit G – Make 4				
	Dark	1	2 ¼" x 4"	
	Light	2,4,6,8,10	2 ¾" x 2 ¾"	◻
	Dark	3,5,7,9	2 ¾" x 2 ¾"	◻
	Light	11	9 ½" x 9 ½"	◻
Unit H – Make 4				
	Dark	1	2 ¼" x 4"	
	Light	2,4,6,8,10	2 ¾" x 2 ¾"	◻
	Dark	3,5,7,9,11	2 ¾" x 2 ¾"	◻
Units I & J – Make 4 each				
	Light	1,3,5,7	2 ¾" x 2 ¾"	◻
	Dark	2,4,6	2 ¾" x 2 ¾"	◻
	Dark	8	5 ¼" x 5 ¼"	◻
Unit K – Make 4				
	Light	1	7 ½" x 7 ½"	

See patterns on pages 95 and 98.

Three blocks shown.

Cutting Instructions:

When making the blocks, either coordinate the fabrics so each block has the same fabric or make them scrappy. I coordinated the fabrics.

From the various light fabrics, cut:

22 – 2" strips. Cut the strips into 1 ¾" x 2" rectangles for a total of 480.

48 – Triangles using Template A for position #16 (left side)

48 – Triangles using Template A reversed for position #17 (right side)

From the various dark fabrics, cut:

24 – 2" strips. (Each strip will supply fabric for 2 blocks.)

Sub-cut the strips into:
    2 – 2" x 6" rectangles for a total of 48
    2 – 2" x 5" rectangles for a total of 48
    2 – 2" x 4" rectangles for a total of 48
    4 – 2" x 3" rectangles for a total of 96

Follow the directions on page 56 for cutting using the template.

See pattern on page 99.

* How to use the border template:

Use the template A that is provided to make a template out of template plastic or the cardboard from a cereal box. Place freezer tape rolled to make double-sided on the back of the template to keep the fabric from moving. Place the template on the straight of grain (see diagram) and make sure the fabric is folded with the wrong sides together so there will be a left side (#16) and a right side (#17) when cutting with the template. Reverse the template to get the optimum use of the fabric. Make sure there is at least ¼" around the template.

Place the Add-A-Quarter with the lip side butted up to the template and cut using a rotary cutter.

Place the bias edge of the template A fabric along the trimmed edge of the block for unit #16. Sew into place and press. Do the same for the template A reversed for unit #17.

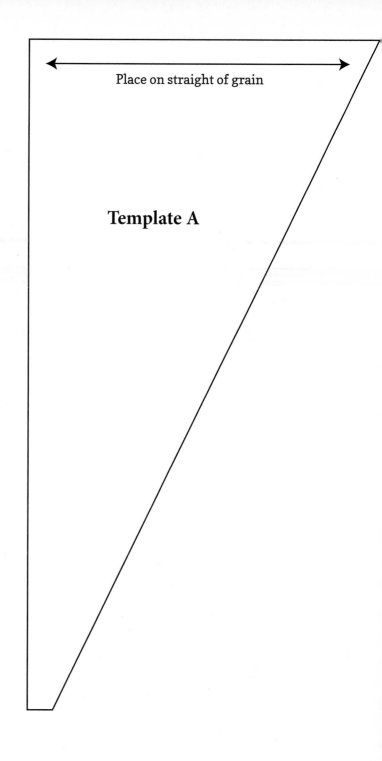

Template A

Place on straight of grain

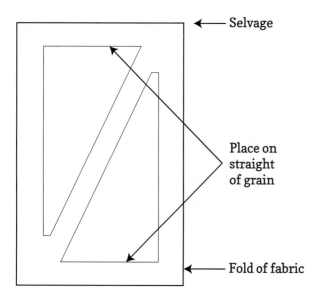

Selvage

Place on straight of grain

Fold of fabric

	Fabric	Position	Size
Unit A – Make 48			
	Dark	1	2" x 3"
	Light	2,3,5,6,8,9, 11,12,14,15	1 ¾" x 2"
	Dark	4	2" x 3"
	Dark	7	2" x 4"
	Dark	10	2" x 5"
	Dark	13	2" x 6"
	Light	16,17	**Follow directions for template

FEATHERED STAR QUILT FINISHING INSTRUCTIONS

Sewing Instructions:

Follow the cutting and position directions to make all the blocks.

Corner Triangles:

From the solid black fabric, cut:

2 – 17 ⅞" squares. Cut each of the squares from corner to corner once on the diagonal.

Sew a triangle onto each corner of center block. Press toward the dark. Remove the paper from the center of the quilt.

First Border:

From the light fabric, cut:

2 – 1 ¾" x 34 ½" strips - Sew on the top and bottom of quilt, press to the dark.

2 – 1 ¾" x 37" strips - Sew on the sides and press to the dark.

Second Border:

From the solid black fabric, cut:

2 – 3 ¼" x 37" strips - Sew on to the top and bottom of the quilt, press to the dark.

2 – 3 ¼" x 42 ½" strips - Sew on to the sides and press to the dark.

Sashing Strips:

From the solid black fabric, cut:

6 – 2" strips. Cut the strips into 16 – 2" x 12 ½" strips. You will have fabric left over.

Arrange the blocks around the center of quilt. Sew the 2" x 12 ½" strips between blocks as shown. Sew the blocks into strips. Sew the top and bottom strips to the center of the quilt, press towards the dark border. Sew the side strips to the quilt, press towards the dark border.

Third Border:

From the solid black fabric, cut:

8 – 3 ½" strips. Sew the border strips together to make:

>2 – 3 ½" x 66 ½" strips - Sew the strips to the top and bottom of the quilt, press to the dark.

>2 – 3 ½" x 72 ½" strips – Sew to the sides of the quilt, press to the dark.

Remove the paper from the blocks.

Pieced Border:

Follow the directions on page 55 to make 48 border blocks.

Cornerstones:

From the solid black fabric, cut:

4 – 6 ½" squares.

Follow the diagram to sew the pieced border and cornerstones into rows. Before sewing the pieced border to the quilt, sew a ⅛" (a stay stitch) around the outside edge of the borders. This will help keep the border from waffling.

Outside Edge:

Sew the top and bottom pieced border to the quilt, press to the dark border. Sew the sides to the quilt, press to the dark border. Remove the paper from the border being careful not to stretch the outside edge. Layer with batting and quilt as desired. Trim off the excess fabric and batting.

Outside edge →

Binding:

From the solid black fabric, cut:

9 – 2 ¼" strips - Sew strips together, fold in half lengthwise and attach to the quilt.

MORNING STARS

Made by Carolyn Cullinan McCormick
Quilted by Carol Willey, Castle Rock, Colo.

HOW TO PAPER PIECE

Why paper piece?

Paper piecing is great for beginners as well as experienced quilters. One can make a wonderful quilt on their very first try since complicated patterns are broken down into easily managed steps. Sewing the fabric to paper makes matching points relatively easy and the paper stabilizes the fabric, enabling one to use even the smallest of scraps.

Get Ready...

1. Use a copy machine to copy your pattern. Make all of your copies from the same original and use the same copy machine. All copy machines distort to some extent so check your pattern by holding the original and the copy together with a light source behind the two sheets of paper. Make as many copies as necessary. It's nice to have a few extras in case you make an error. Use the lightest weight paper you can find. The heavier the paper, the more difficult it is to remove.

2. Set up your sewing machine. Use a 90/14 size needle and set the stitch length to 18 – 20 stitches per inch. The larger needle perforates the paper making it easier to tear off. The smaller stitches keep the seams from ripping out when you remove the paper.

3. Place a piece of muslin or scrap fabric on your ironing board. When you press the pieces, the ink from the copies can transfer onto your ironing board cover. **Caution:** Please be aware that the dye in dye-based inks in ink-jet printers will dissolve when exposed to water, thus there is a possibility for the ink to transfer onto your fabric when using steam for pressing. Pigmented inks are more water resistant than dye-based inks. Please check to make sure that your ink does not dissolve when exposed to water.

4. Make sure you have a light source nearby. The light on your sewing machine is usually adequate.

5. Remember when paper piecing your pattern will be reversed.

Get Set...

1. Here is a familiar pattern ... see **Fig. A.** Instead of templates with seam allowances as many of us are used to seeing, we have lines and numbers. The lines indicate where to sew and the numbers indicate the sequence in which to sew. The only seam allowances that are shown are the ones that go around either a block or a unit.

2. The front of the pattern is where the lines and numbers are printed. This is the side you will sew on.

3. The back of the pattern is the side that is blank. This is where your fabric will be placed.

4. Cut your fabric pieces by following the cutting chart for each block. Always make sure the pieces of fabric are at least one-quarter of an inch larger all the way around than shown on the foundation pattern.

Sew!

1. Put fabric number 1 **RIGHT SIDE UP** on the blank side of the pattern. You may either pin the piece in place or use double-sided tape to hold the fabric in place. The tape makes the fabric lie flat on the paper. The pin can make a small rise in the paper. See **Fig. B.**

2. Turn the foundation pattern over, look through the paper towards your light source and make sure the fabric extends over the lines on each side by at least one-quarter of an inch. See **Fig. C.**

3. Place an index card or template plastic on the sewing line between piece number 1 and piece number 2. Fold back the foundation pattern over

the edge of the card. You can now see the excess fabric from piece number 1. See **Fig. D.**

4. Place the Add-A-Quarter ruler up against the fold of the foundation paper with lip side down. Use the rotary cutter to trim the extra fabric from piece number 1. You will now have a straight line to help you place fabric piece number 2. See **Fig. E.**

5. Now place the fabric that goes in position number 2 of the pattern on the trimmed edge of piece number 1 with the right sides facing each other. See **Fig. F.**

6. Turn the foundation paper over and stitch on the line between piece number 1 and piece number 2. Sew a few stitches before the line begins and a few stitches after the line ends. Make sure piece number 2 does not slip. See **Fig. G.**

7. Flip the paper back over and open piece number 2. Press the piece open using a dry iron. See **Fig. H.**

8. Fold the foundation paper back along the line between piece number 1 and piece number 3 using the index card or the template plastic. Butt the Add-A-Quarter up against the paper and trim the excess fabric. See **Fig. I.**

9. Turn the foundation back over and position fabric piece number 3, being careful not to displace your fabric. Sew on the line between number 1 and number 3. See **Figs. J & K.**

10. Continue sewing each piece in place in the numeric order given until all the pieces are sewn in place and each unit is complete. See **Fig. L.**

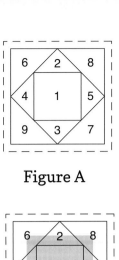

Figure A

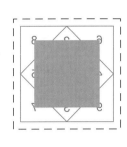

Figure B

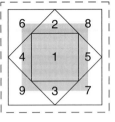

Figure C

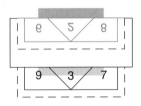

Figure D

Figure E

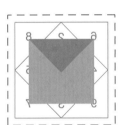

Figure F

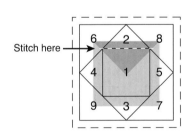

Stitch here →

Figure G

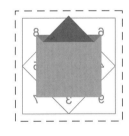

Figure H

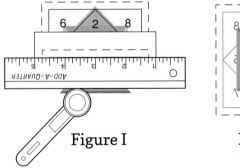

Figure I

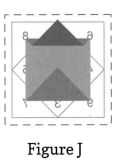

Figure J

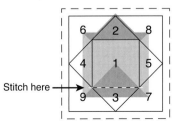

Stitch here →

Figure K

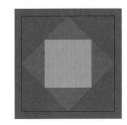

Figure L

After all the pieces are sewn onto the foundation, you will be ready to trim the edges. You will need a ¼" seam allowance around the entire block, no matter the size of the block, when you sew your blocks together. **NEVER TRIM ON THE SOLID LINE!** Line up the ruler with the solid line on the foundation. Trim off the excess fabric using your rotary cutter.

If you are paper piecing a block that is made up of multiple units, the time has come to sew them together. Pin the units together. Make sure the lines you are sewing match on the top and the bottom of the units. This can be accomplished by putting a pin straight through both lines at each intersection. Always check to make sure the seam is directly on the top line and the underneath line as well, otherwise your block will be off.

When the block is finished, **DO NOT REMOVE THE PAPER!** It is best to join the blocks before you remove the paper. This gives you a line to follow when you sew the blocks together. Remove the paper after the blocks are sewn together. You might want to remove the really small pieces with a pair of tweezers.

A few variations...

Since these patterns have been adapted to a paper pieced pattern from traditional blocks, you will have a few things crop up that you might not run into with blocks that were originally designed with paper piecing in mind.

1. You may have triangles that are either sewn to inside or outside corners of the block. These are shown as separated pieces. You may either pin or use double-sided tape to hold your fabric to the triangles. Sew them in the order indicated on the pattern leaving the paper in place.
2. Use half-square triangles where you see this symbol:

Just a few suggestions...

1. If you have to unsew and the paper foundation separates on the sewing line, use a piece of clear tape to repair the pattern. Sometimes you will notice the stitches from the previously sewn fabric when you fold back the foundation. If this happens, just pull the foundation away from the fabric and trim using the ruler.

2. After you have sewn two units together and pressed, remove the paper from the back side of the seam allowance to reduce some of the bulk.

3. To help speed up your paper piecing, place all of your position 1 pieces on multiple units at the same time. Trim and sew multiple units at the same time.

4. By placing your pattern face down on a white piece of paper you will be able to see the outline of the design for placement of your first fabric.

PAPER PIECING PATTERNS

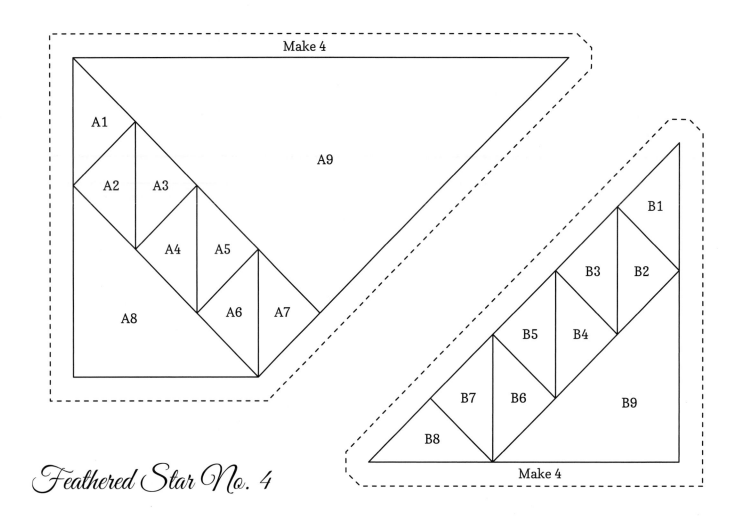

Make 4

A1
A2 A3
A4 A5
A8 A6 A7
A9

B1
B3 B2
B5 B4
B7 B6
B8 B9

Make 4

Feathered Star No. 4

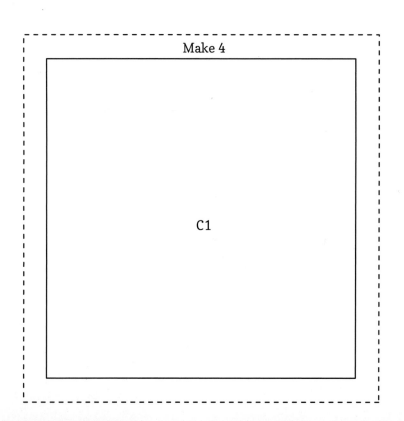

Make 4

C1

Feathered Star No. 4

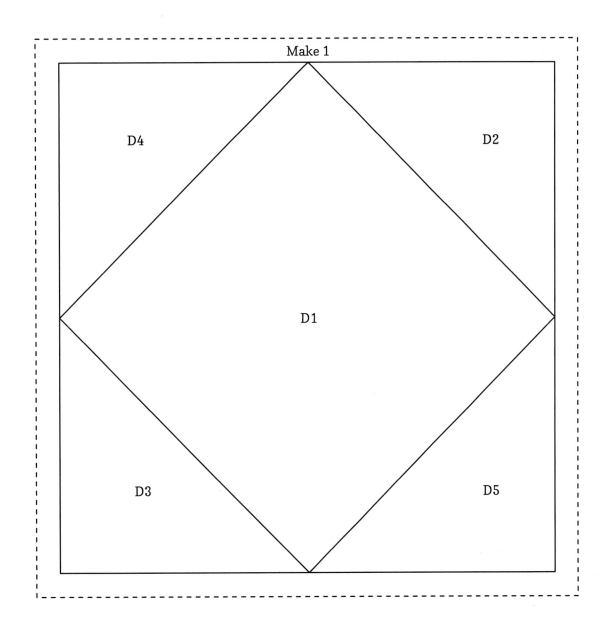

Make 1

D4

D2

D1

D3

D5

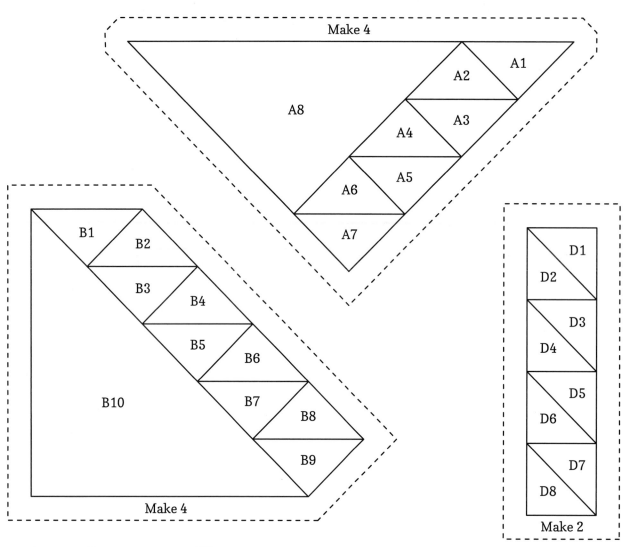

Make 4

A1
A2
A3
A4
A5
A6
A7
A8

Make 4

B1
B2
B3
B4
B5
B6
B7
B8
B9
B10

Make 2

D1
D2
D3
D4
D5
D6
D7
D8

The Twinkling Star

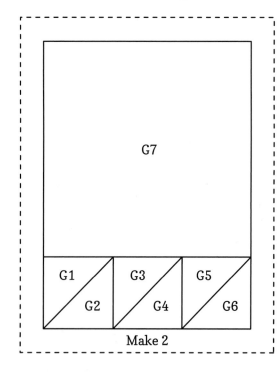

G7

G1
G2
G3
G4
G5
G6

Make 2

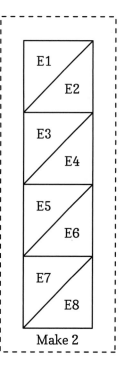

E1
E2
E3
E4
E5
E6
E7
E8

Make 2

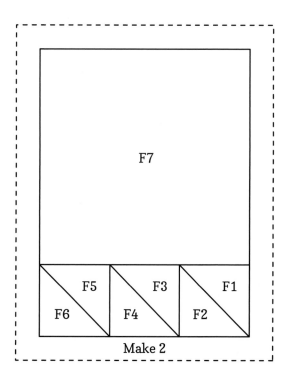

F7

F5
F6
F3
F4
F1
F2

Make 2

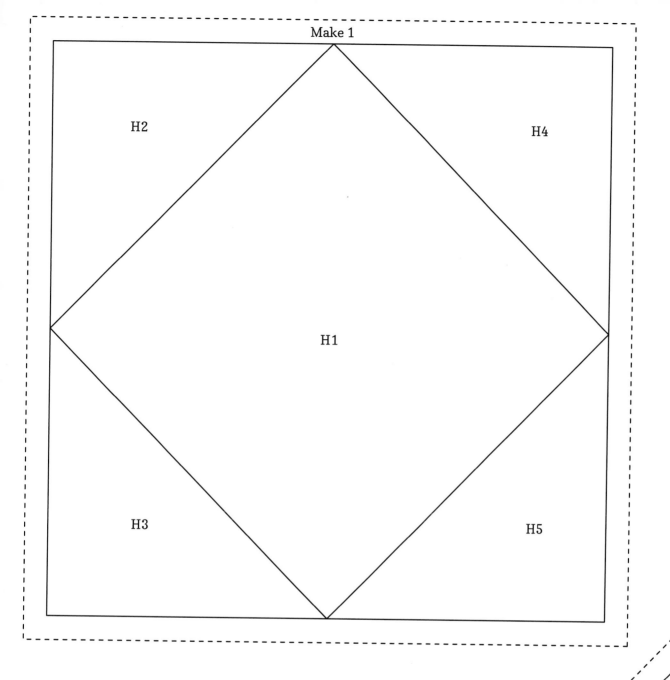

Make 1

H2

H4

H1

H3

H5

The Twinkling Star

C1

Make 4

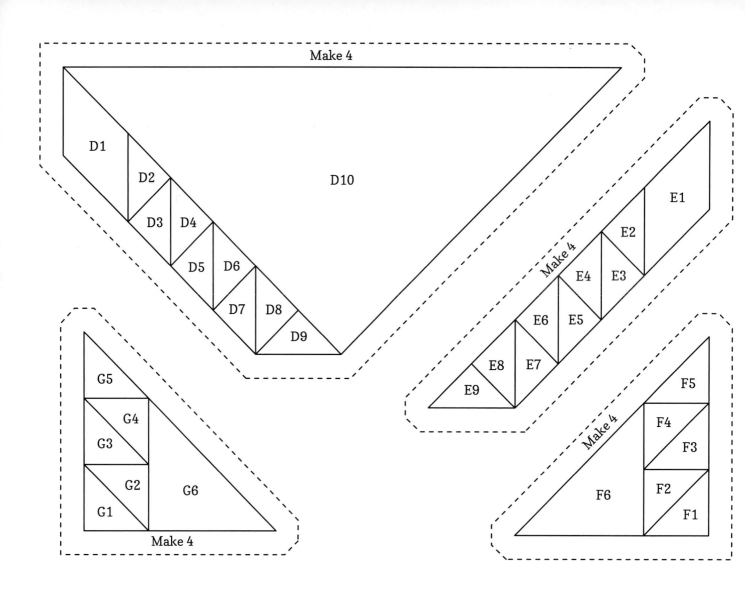

Make 4

D1
D2
D3 D4
D5 D6
D7 D8
D9
D10

Make 4

E1
E2
E4 E3
E6 E5
E8 E7
E9

Make 4

G5
G4
G3
G2
G1 G6

Make 4

Make 4

F5
F4
F3
F2
F1
F6

Feathered Edge Star

Make 4

H1

Feathered Edge Star

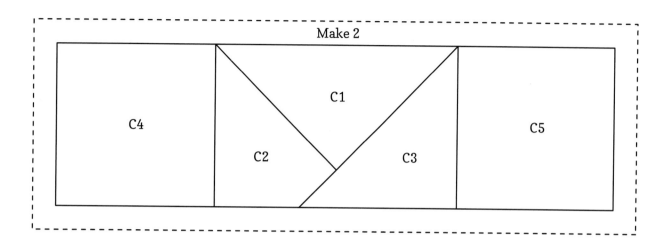

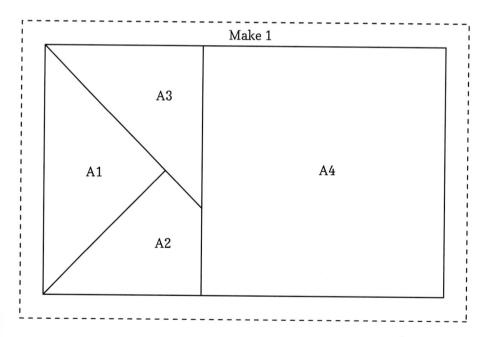

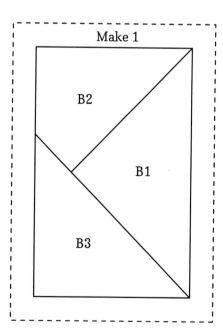

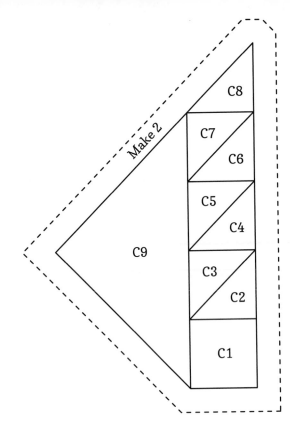

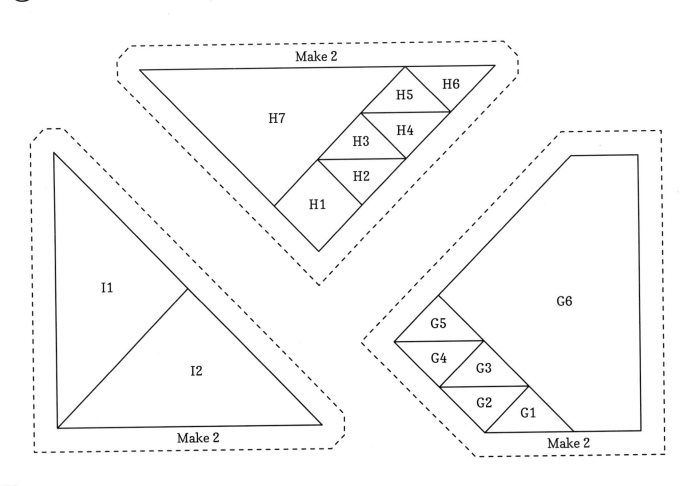

Feathered Star No. 5

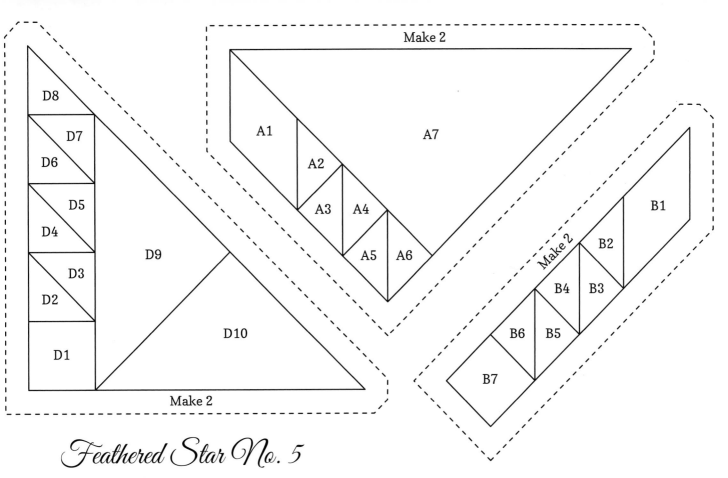

Feathered Star No. 5

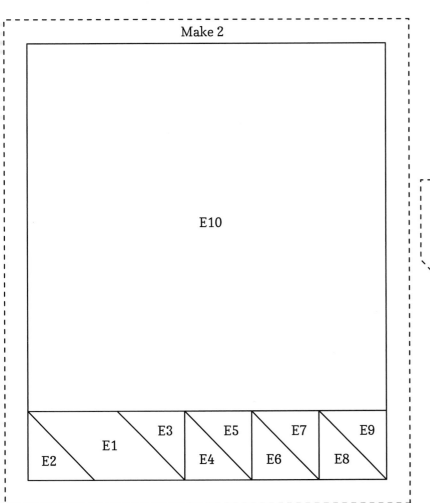

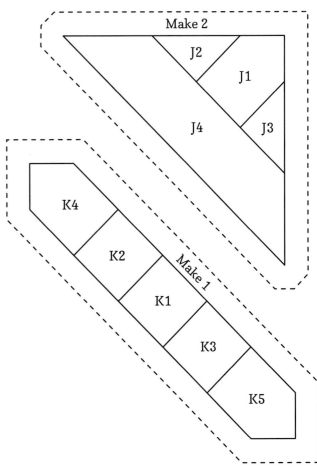

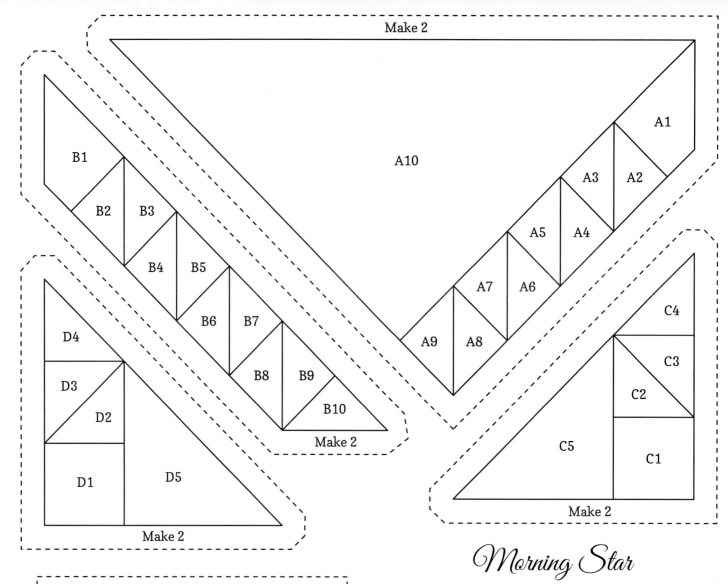

Make 2

B1
B2 B3
B4 B5
B6 B7
B8 B9
B10

A10

A1
A2
A3 A4
A5 A6
A7 A8
A9

Make 2

D4
D3
D2
D1 D5

Make 2

C4
C3
C2
C5 C1

Make 2

Morning Star

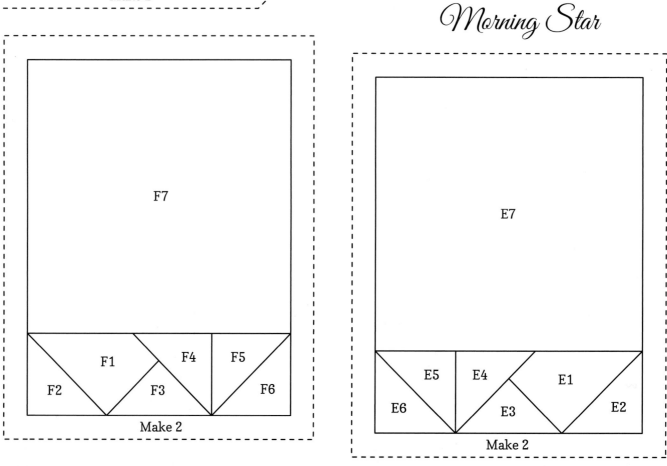

F7

F1 F4 F5
F2 F3 F6

Make 2

E7

E5 E4 E1
E6 E3 E2

Make 2

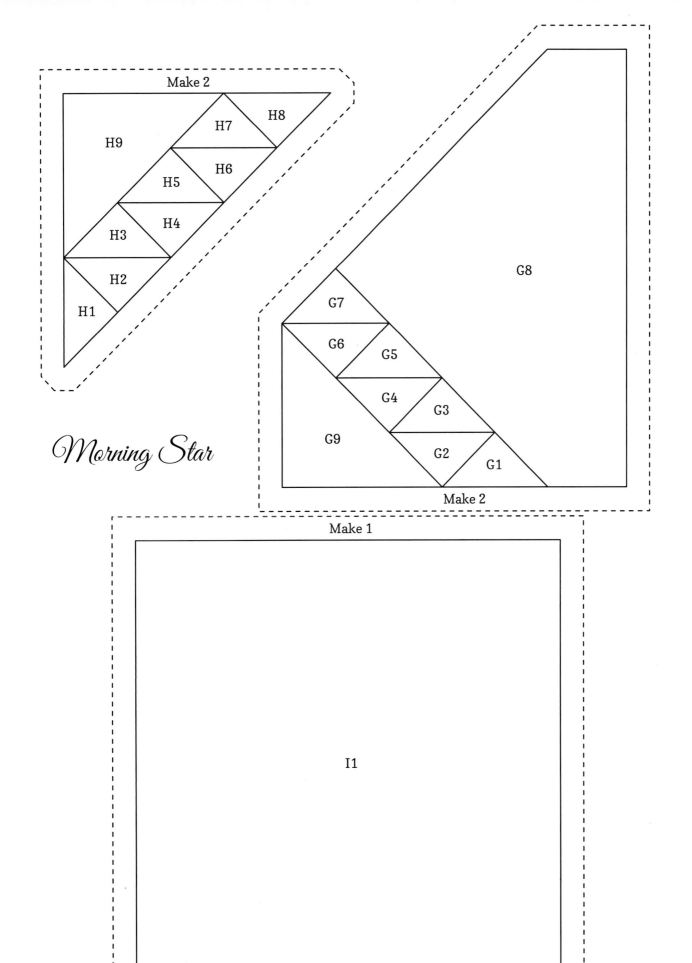

Make 2

H9
H7
H8
H5
H6
H3
H4
H2
H1

Morning Star

G8
G7
G6
G5
G4
G3
G9
G2
G1

Make 2

Make 1

I1

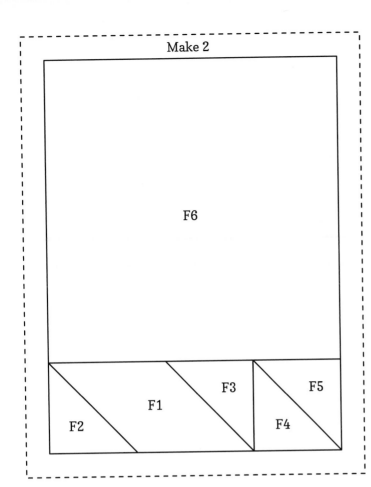

Make 2

F6

F1
F2
F3
F4
F5

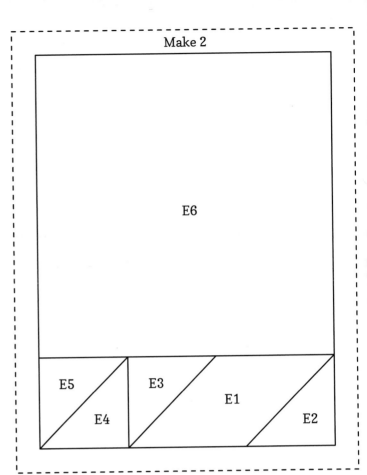

Make 2

E6

E5
E4
E3
E1
E2

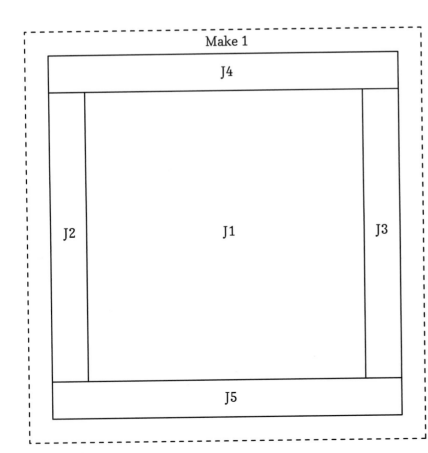

Make 1

J4

J2

J1

J3

J5

Star-of-Chamblie

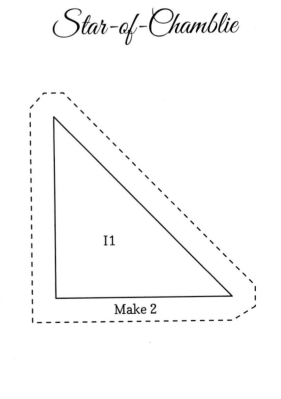

I1

Make 2

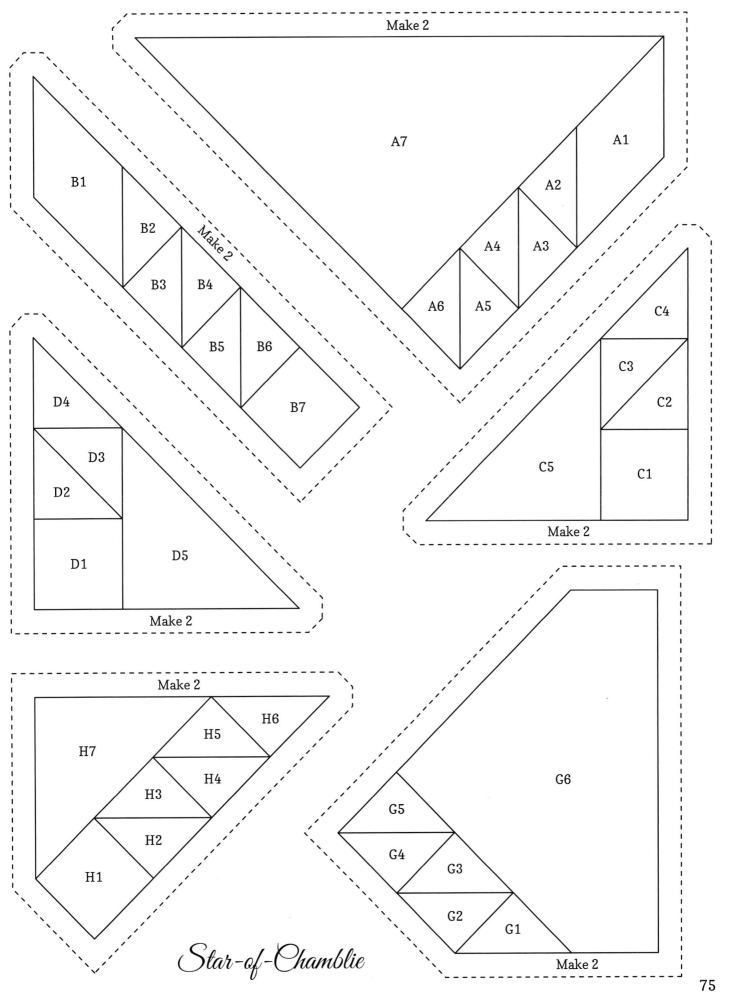

Make 2

A7

A1

A2

A4 A3

A6 A5

B1

B2

B3 B4

Make 2

B5 B6

B7

C4

C3

C2

C5 C1

Make 2

D4

D3

D2

D1 D5

Make 2

Make 2

H6

H5

H7

H4

H3

H2

H1

G6

G5

G4

G3

G2

G1

Make 2

Star-of-Chamblie

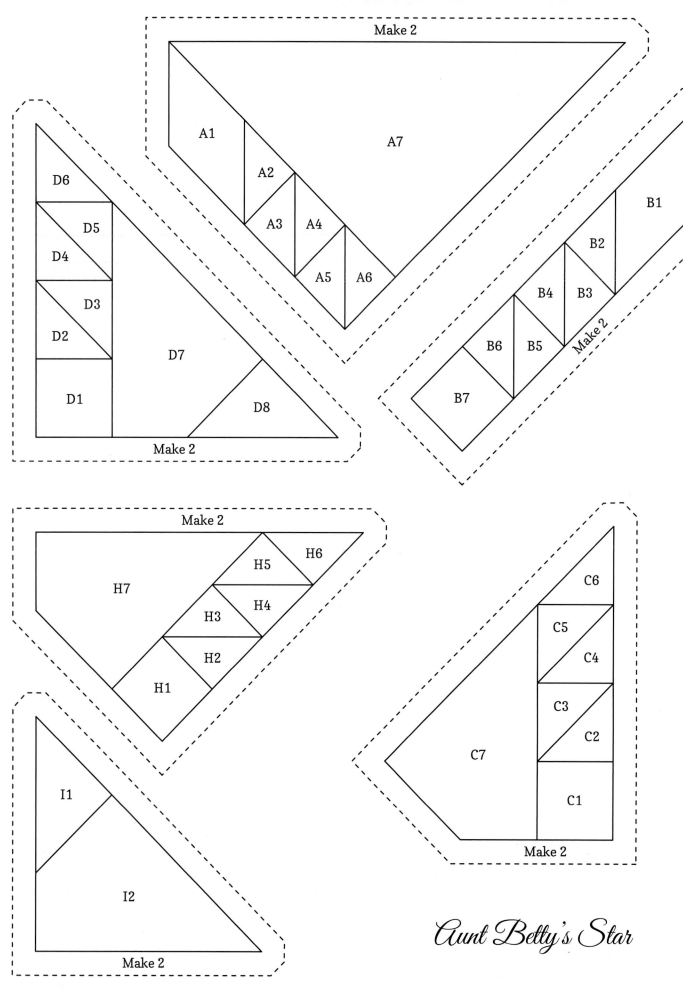

Make 2

A1
A2
A3 A4
A5 A6
A7

D6
D5
D4
D3
D2
D1
D7
D8

Make 2

B1
B2
B3
B4
B5
B6
B7

Make 2

Make 2

H7
H6
H5
H4
H3
H2
H1

C6
C5
C4
C3
C2
C7
C1

Make 2

I1
I2

Make 2

Aunt Betty's Star

Aunt Betty's Star

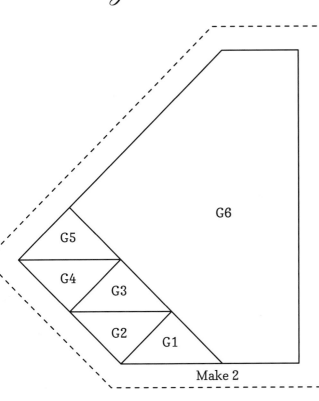

G6

G5

G4

G3

G2

G1

Make 2

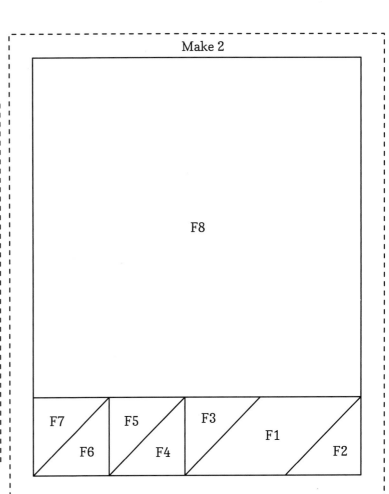

Make 2

F8

F7
F6
F5
F4
F3
F1
F2

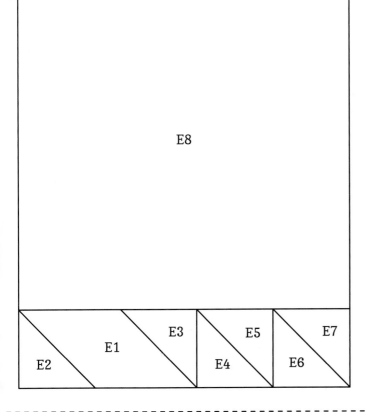

Make 2

E8

E3
E2
E1
E5
E4
E7
E6

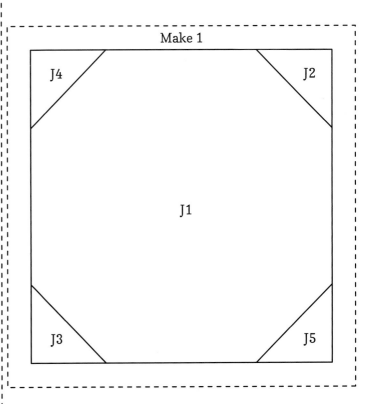

Make 1

J4
J2
J1
J3
J5

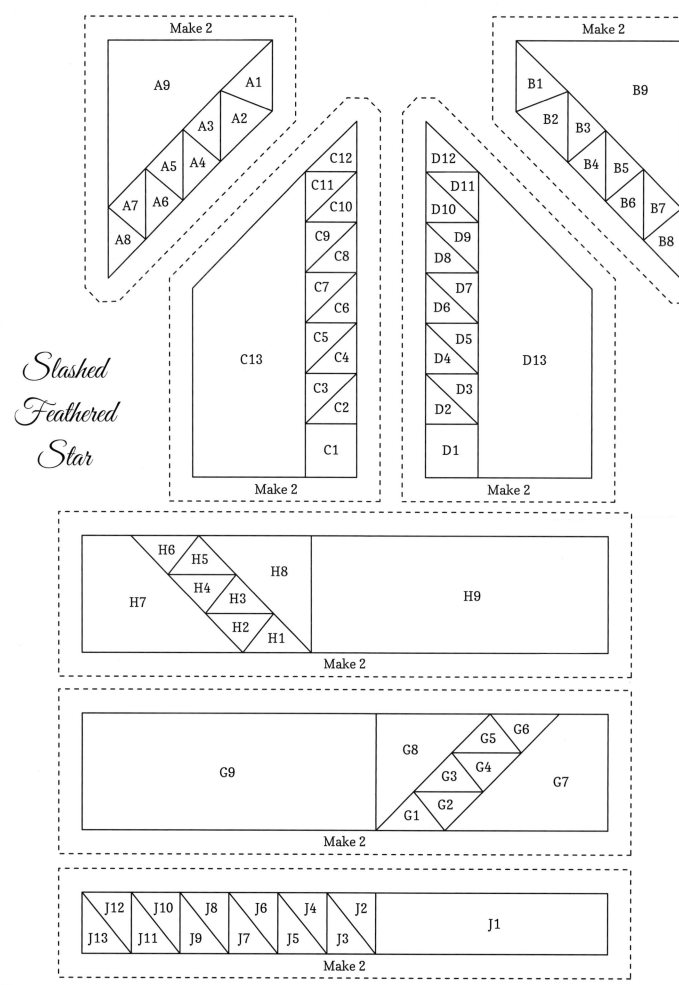

Slashed
Feathered
Star

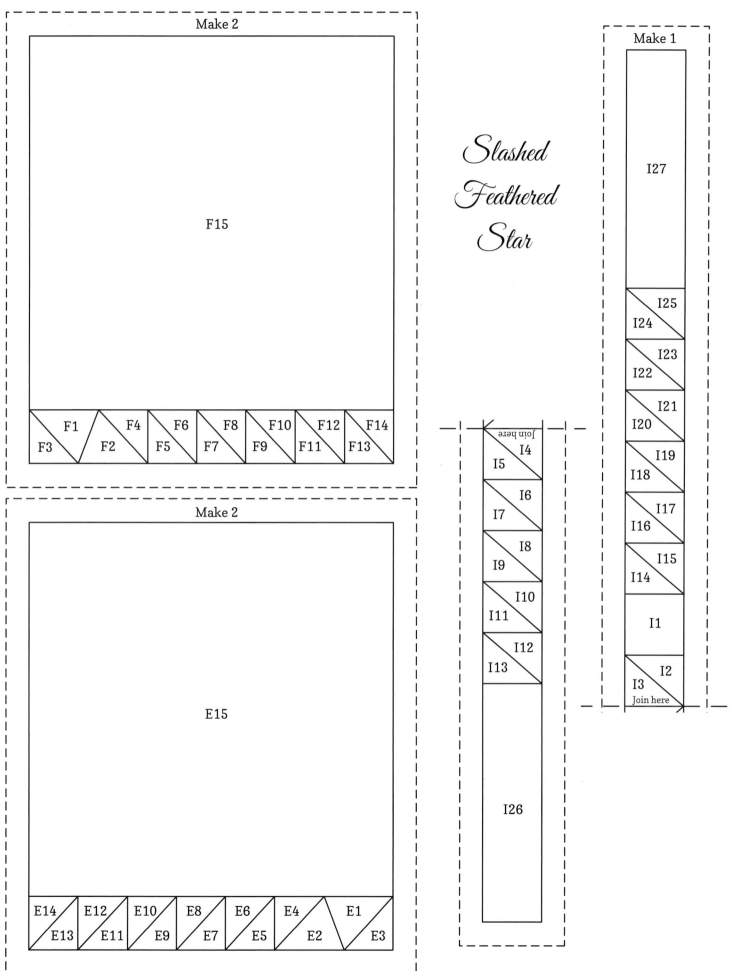

Slashed
Feathered
Star

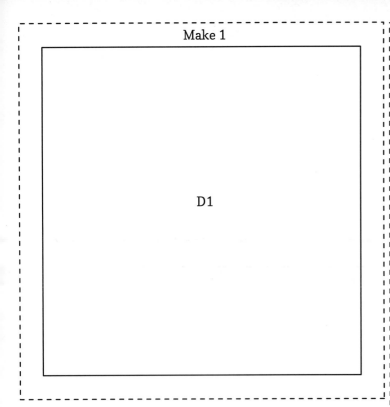

Make 1

D1

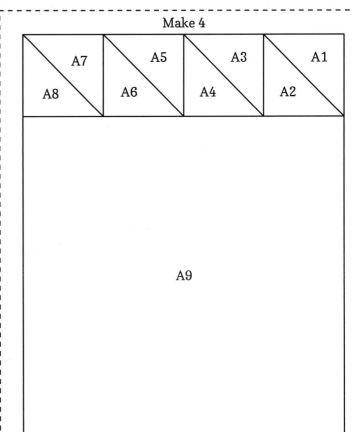

Make 4

A7 A5 A3 A1
A8 A6 A4 A2

A9

Feathered Star No. 2

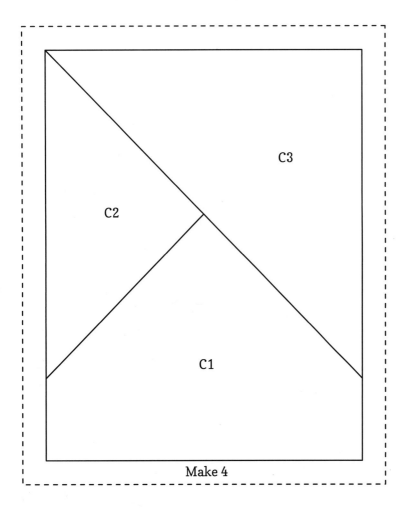

C3

C2

C1

Make 4

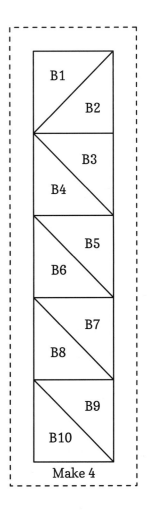

B1
B2
B3
B4
B5
B6
B7
B8
B9
B10

Make 4

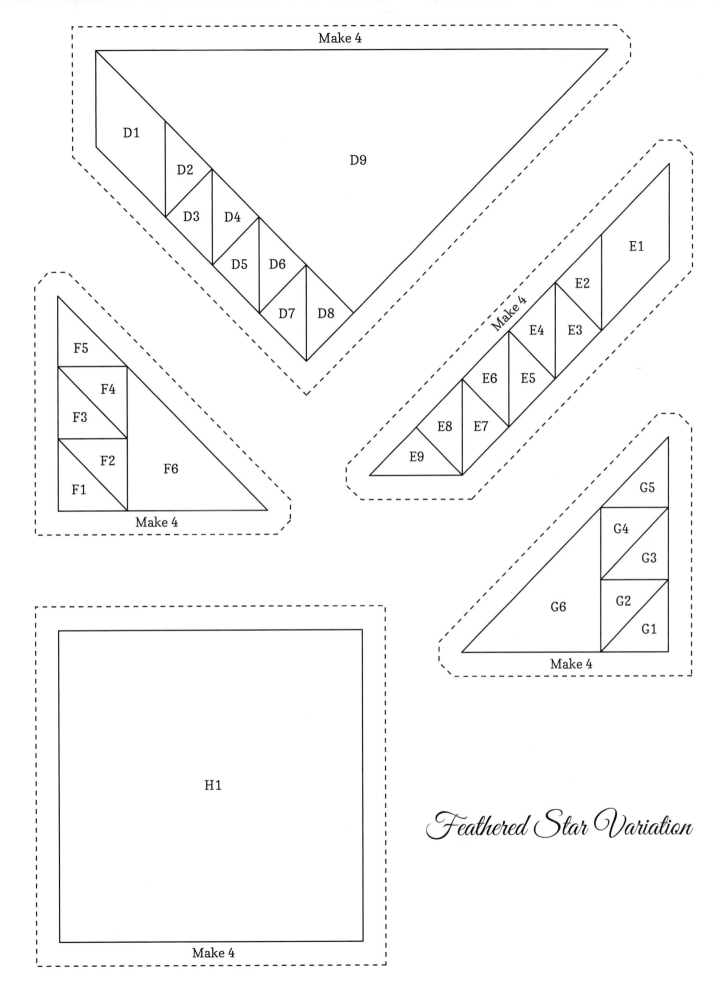

Make 4

D1

D2

D3 D4

D5 D6

D7 D8

D9

E1

E2

E3

E4

E5

E6

E7

E8

E9

Make 4

F5

F4

F3

F2

F1

F6

Make 4

G5

G4

G3

G2

G1

G6

Make 4

H1

Make 4

Feathered Star Variation

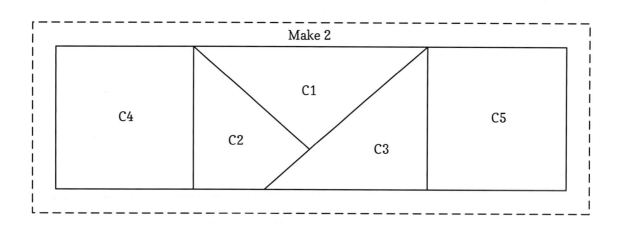

Make 2

C4 · C1 · C2 · C3 · C5

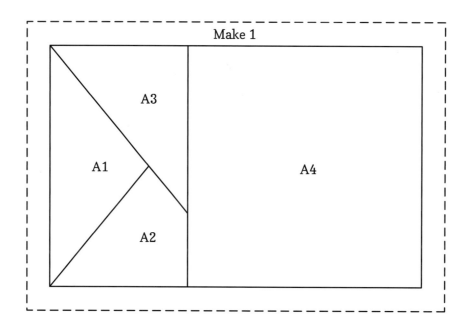

Make 1

A3 · A1 · A2 · A4

Feathered Star
Variation

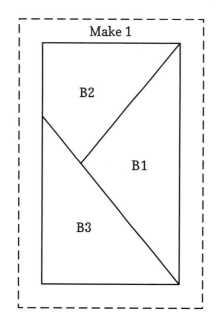

Make 1

B2 · B1 · B3

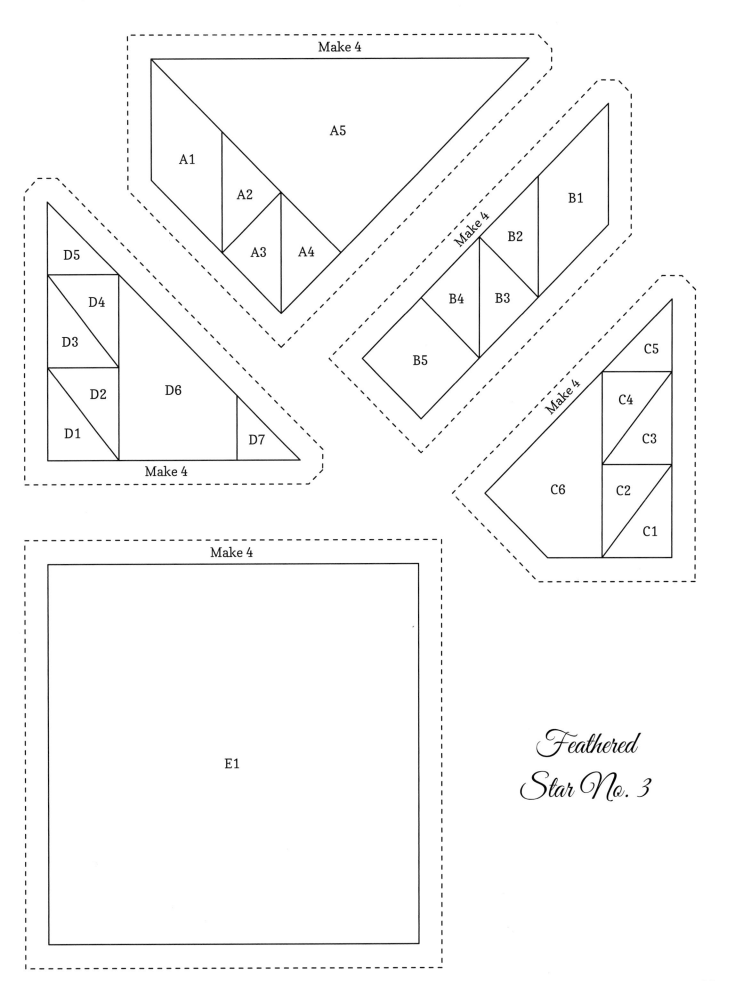

Make 4

A5

A1

A2

A3 A4

B1

B2

Make 4

B4 B3

B5

D5

D4

D3

D2

D1

D6

D7

Make 4

C5

C4

C3

Make 4

C6

C2

C1

E1

Make 4

Feathered Star No. 3

83

Feathered Star No. 3

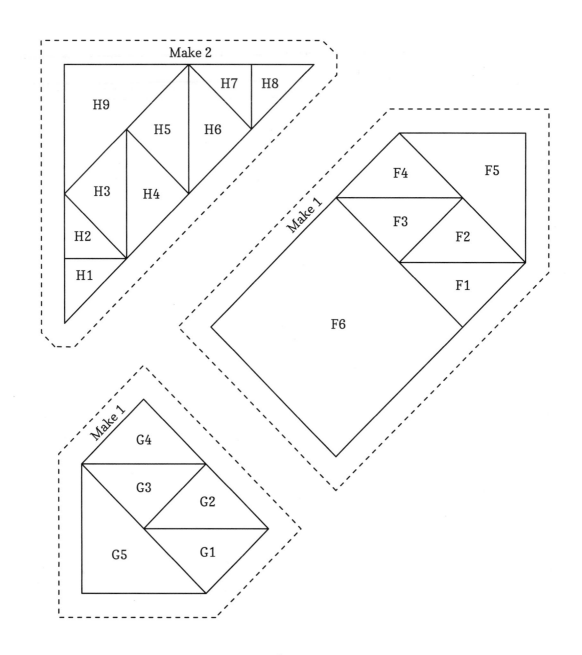

Make 2

H9 H7 H8 H5 H6 H3 H4 H2 H1

Make 1

F4 F5 F3 F2 F1 F6

Make 1

G4 G3 G2 G5 G1

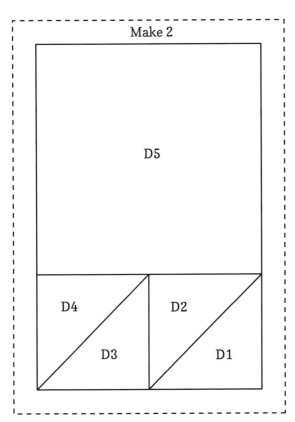

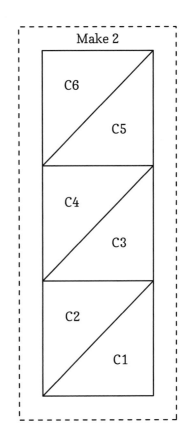

The Hour Glass

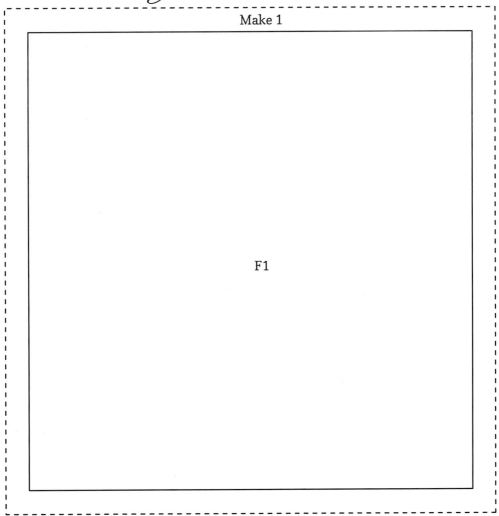

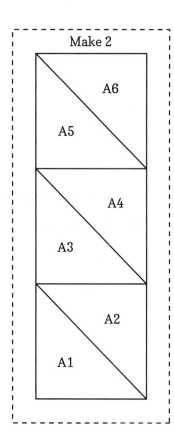

Make 2

A6
A5
A4
A3
A2
A1

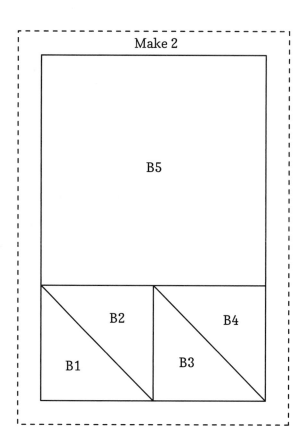

Make 2

B5
B2
B4
B1
B3

The Hour Glass

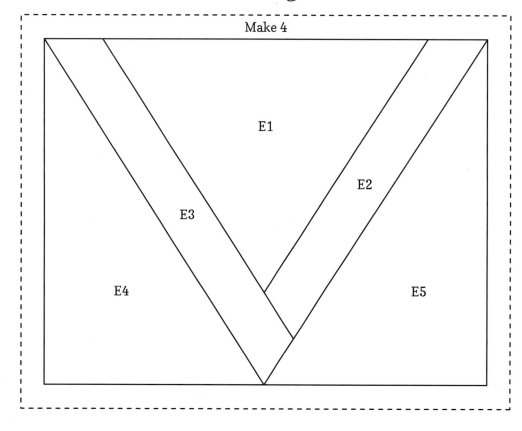

Make 4

E1
E2
E3
E4
E5

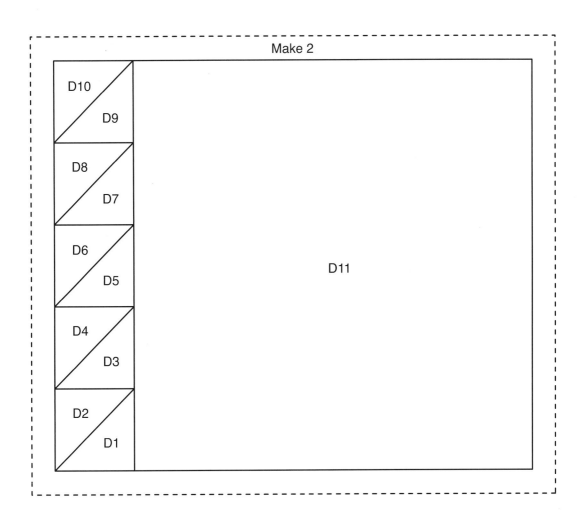

Feathered Star No. 6

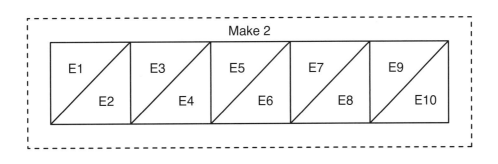

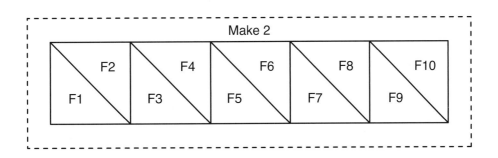

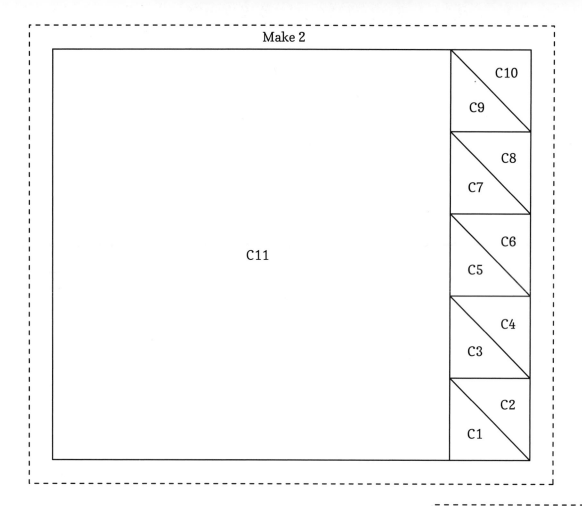

Feathered Star No. 6

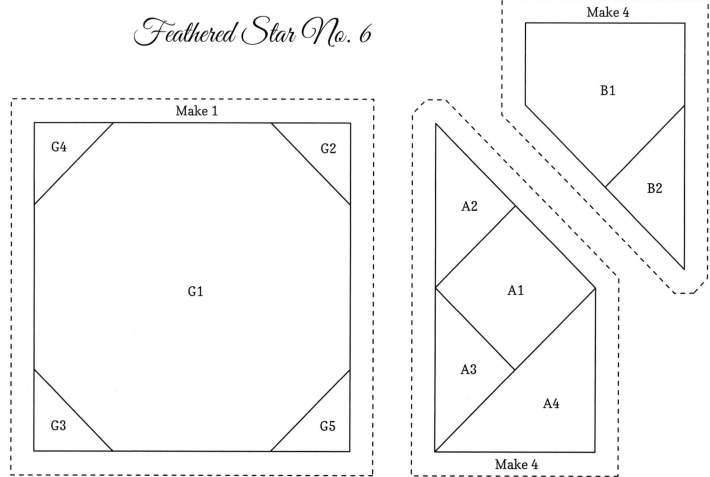

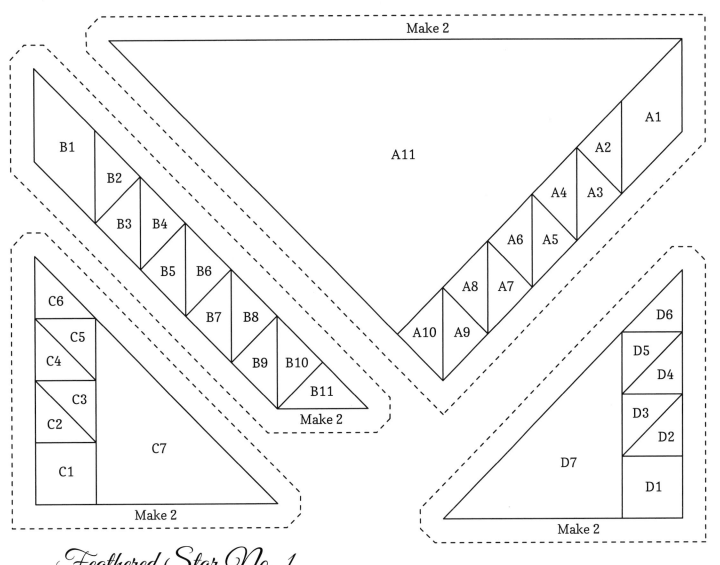

Make 2

B1 B2 B3 B4 B5 B6 B7 B8 B9 B10 B11

A11 A1 A2 A3 A4 A5 A6 A7 A8 A9 A10

Make 2

Make 2

C6 C5 C4 C3 C2 C1 C7

Make 2

D6 D5 D4 D3 D2 D1 D7

Make 2

Feathered Star No. 1

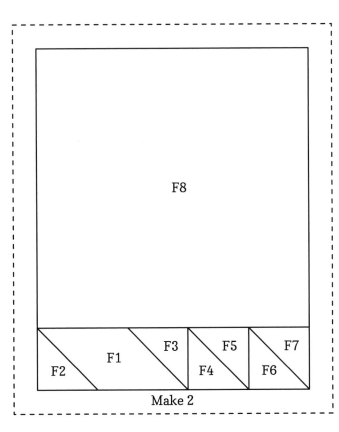

F8 F1 F2 F3 F4 F5 F6 F7

Make 2

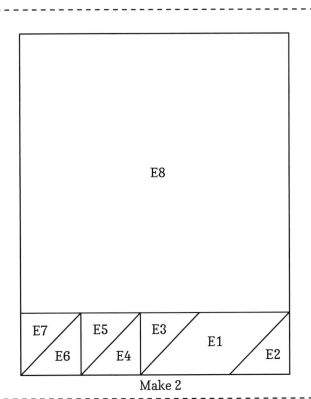

E8 E7 E6 E5 E4 E3 E2 E1

Make 2

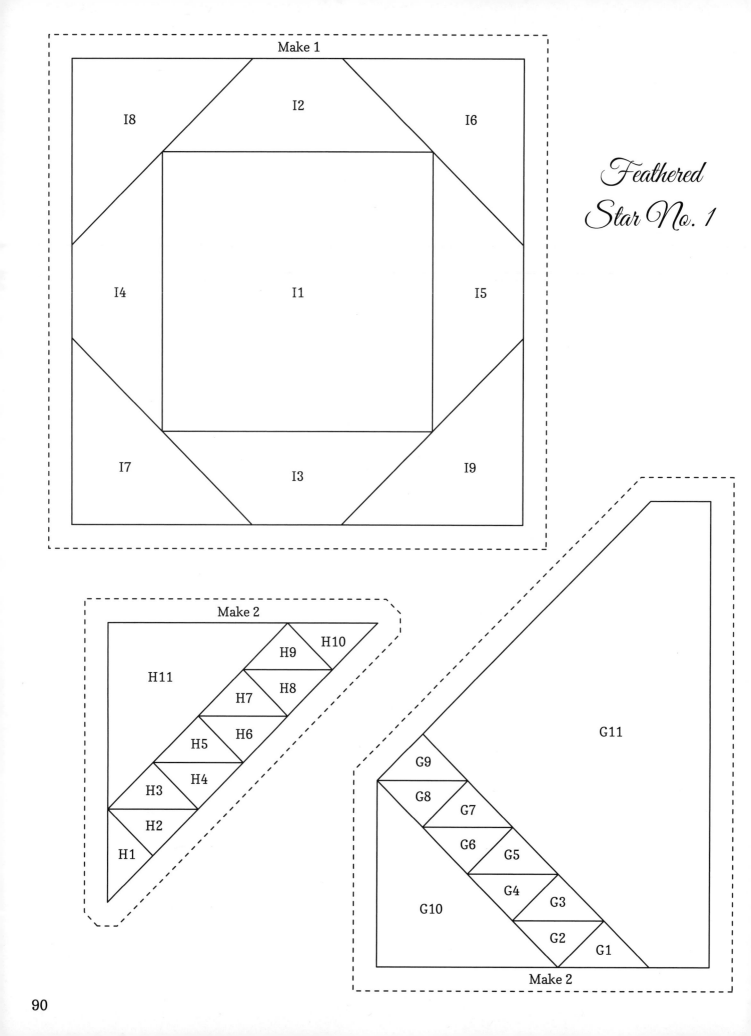

Make 1

I8

I2

I6

I4

I1

I5

I7

I3

I9

*Feathered
Star No. 1*

Make 2

H10
H9
H11
H8
H7
H6
H5
H4
H3
H2
H1

G11

G9
G8
G7
G6
G5
G4
G3
G2
G1
G10

Make 2

90

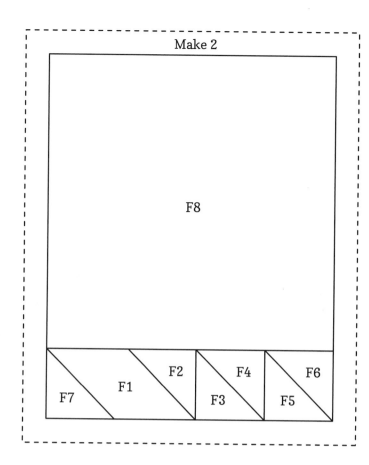

Make 2

F8

F7 | F1 | F2 | F3 | F4 | F5 | F6

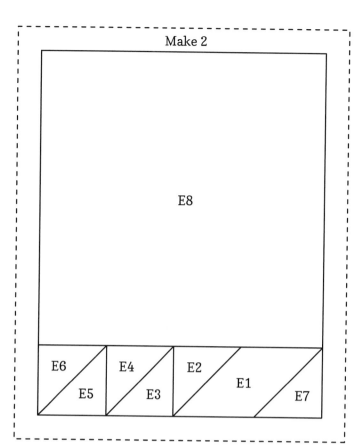

Make 2

E8

E6 | E5 | E4 | E3 | E2 | E1 | E7

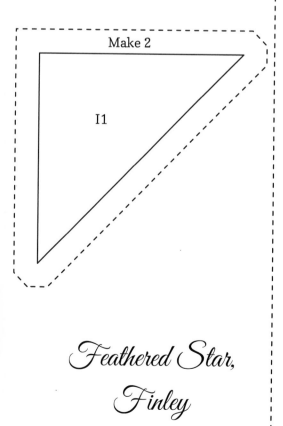

Make 2

I1

Feathered Star,
Finley

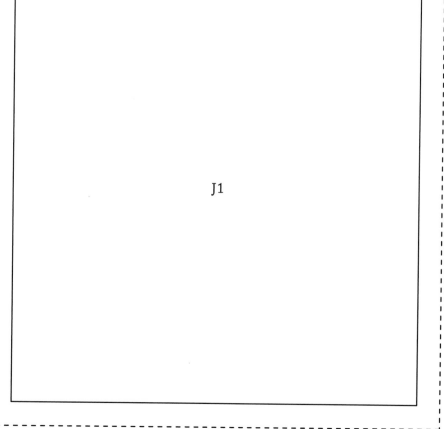

Make 1

J1

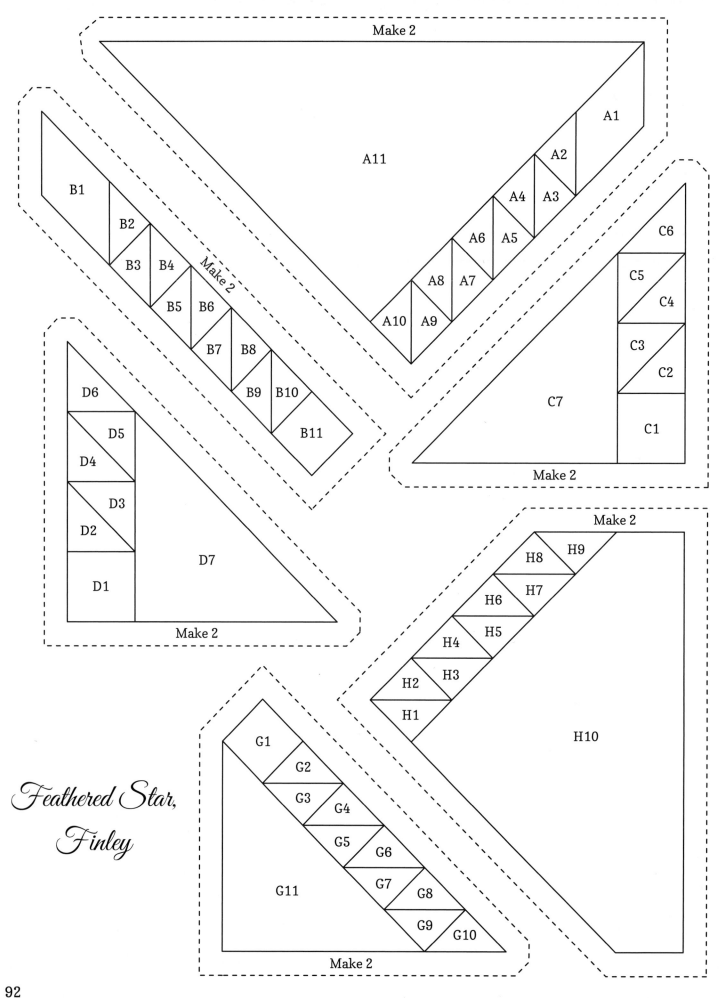

Make 2

A1

A11

A2

A4 A3

A6 A5

A8 A7

A10 A9

B1

B2

B3 B4

Make 2

B5 B6

B7 B8

B9 B10

B11

C6

C5

C4

C3

C2

C7

C1

Make 2

D6

D5

D4

D3

D2

D7

D1

Make 2

Make 2

H8 H9

H6 H7

H4 H5

H2 H3

H1

H10

G1

G2

G3

G4

G5

G6

G7

G8

G9 G10

G11

Feathered Star,
Finley

Make 2

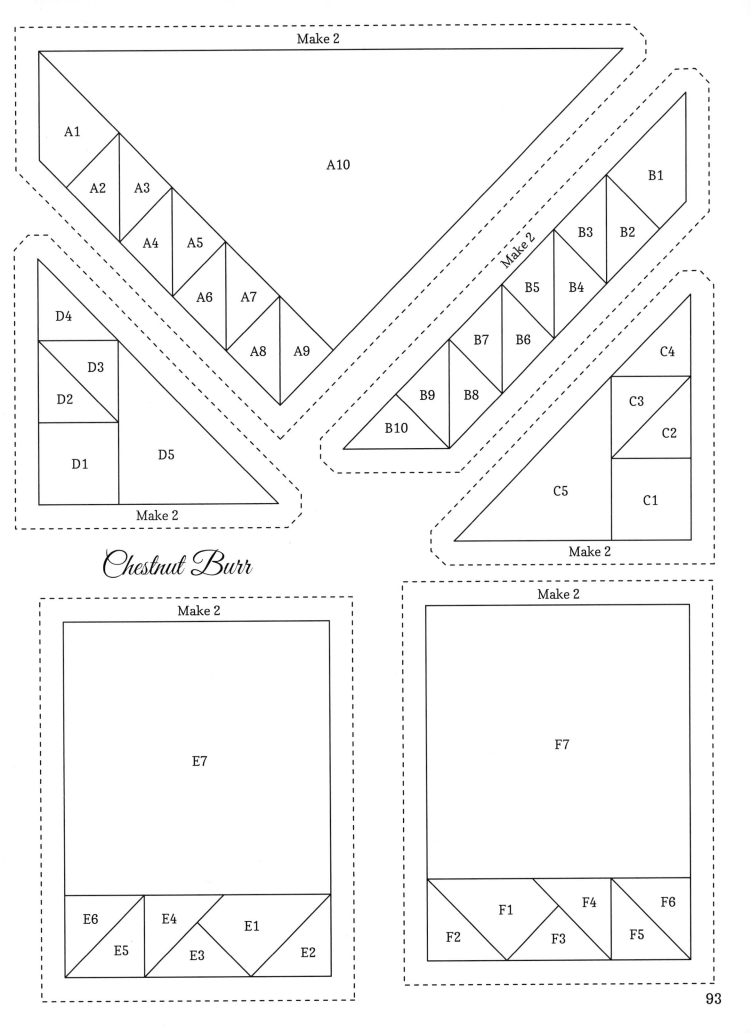

Make 2

A1
A10
A2 A3
A4 A5
A6 A7
A8 A9

B1
B3 B2
B5 B4
Make 2
B7 B6
B9 B8
B10

C4
C3
C2
C5
C1
Make 2

D4
D3
D2
D1
D5
Make 2

Chestnut Burr

Make 2

E7

E6
E5
E4
E3
E1
E2

Make 2

F7

F1
F2
F3
F4
F5
F6

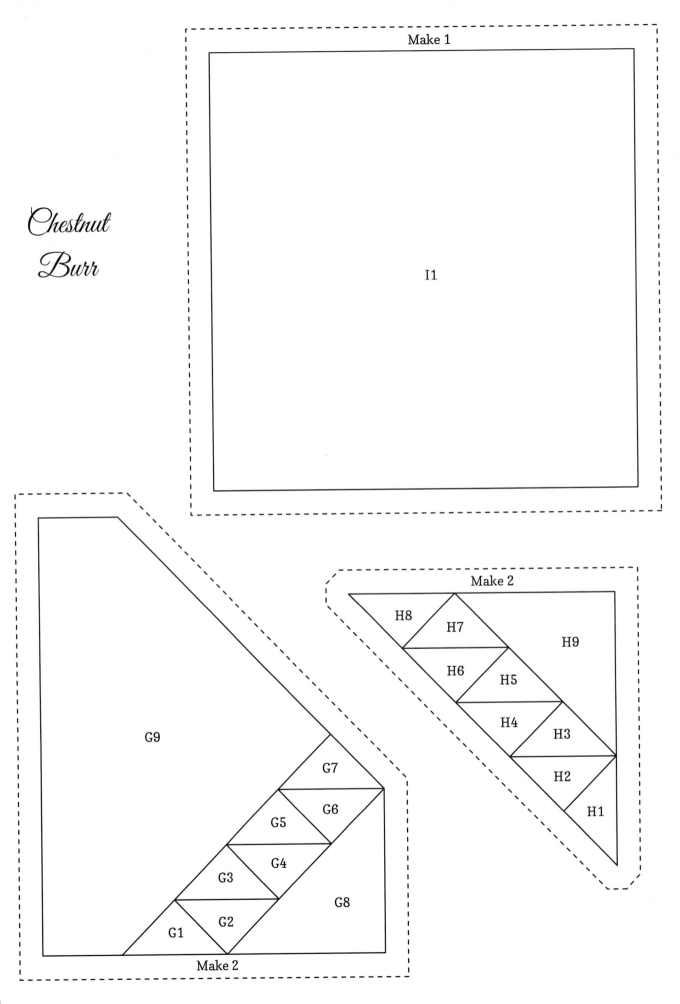

Chestnut Burr

Make 1

I1

Make 2

H8 H7 H9 H6 H5 H4 H3 H2 H1

G9 G7 G6 G5 G4 G3 G8 G2 G1

Make 2

94

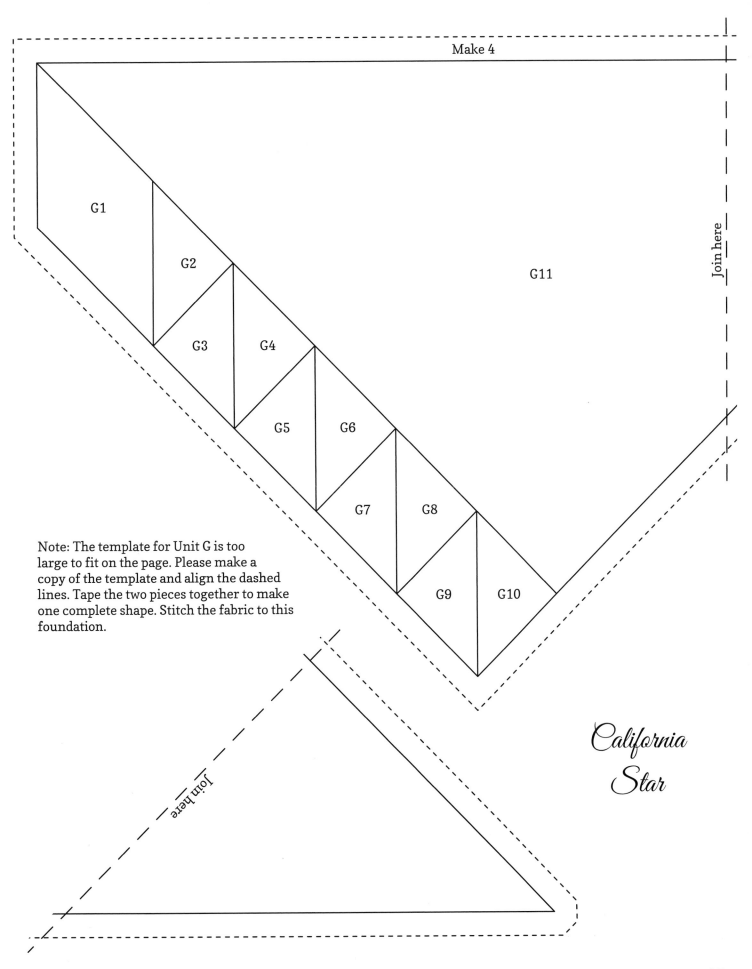

Make 4

Join here

G1

G2

G3

G4

G5

G6

G7

G8

G9

G10

G11

Note: The template for Unit G is too large to fit on the page. Please make a copy of the template and align the dashed lines. Tape the two pieces together to make one complete shape. Stitch the fabric to this foundation.

Join here

California Star

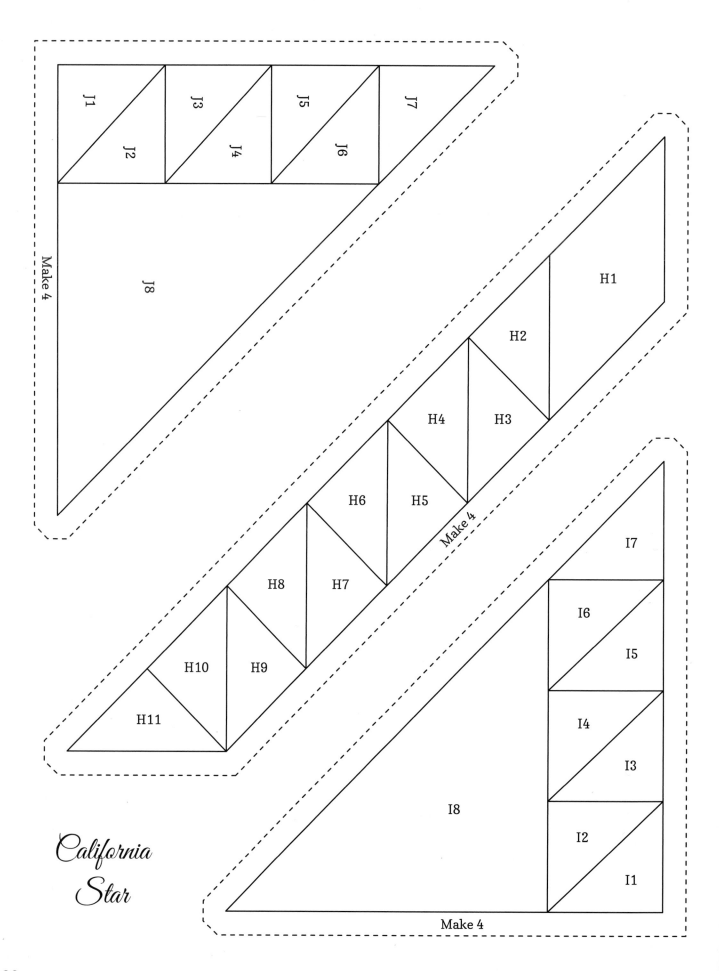

Make 4

J1
J2
J3
J4
J5
J6
J7
J8

H1
H2
H3
H4
H5
H6
H7
H8
H9
H10
H11

Make 4

I1
I2
I3
I4
I5
I6
I7
I8

Make 4

California
Star

California Star

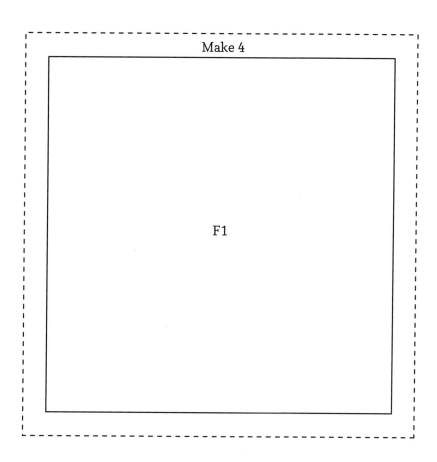

Make 4

F1

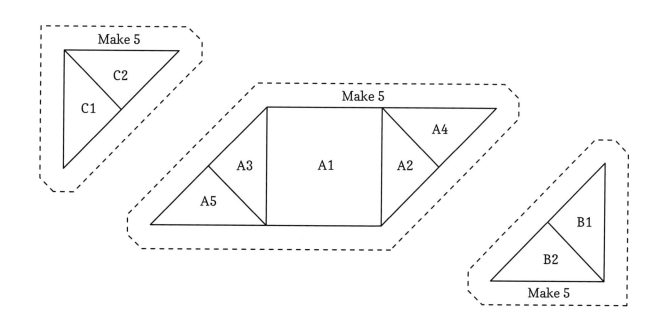

Make 5

C2

C1

Make 5

A4

A3

A1

A2

A5

B1

B2

Make 5

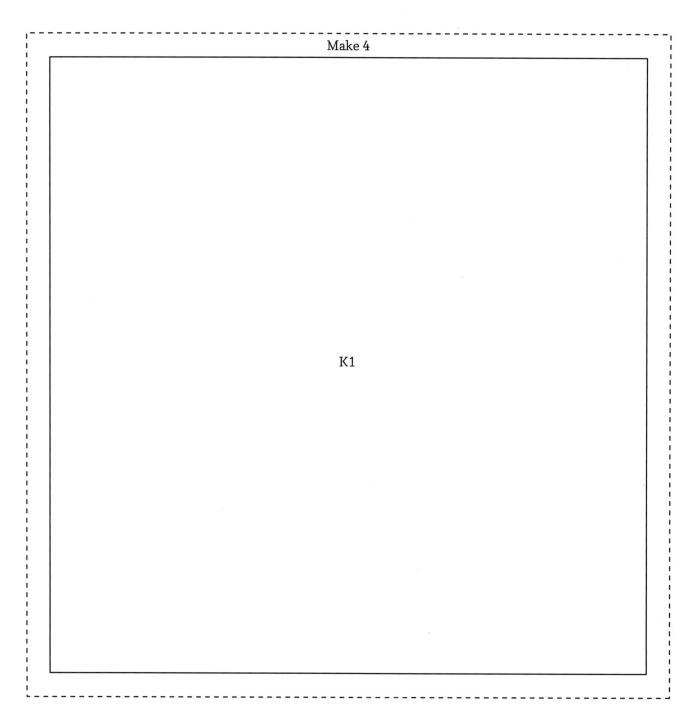

Make 4

K1

Make 10

E3   E2   E1

Make 10

D1   D2   D3

California Star

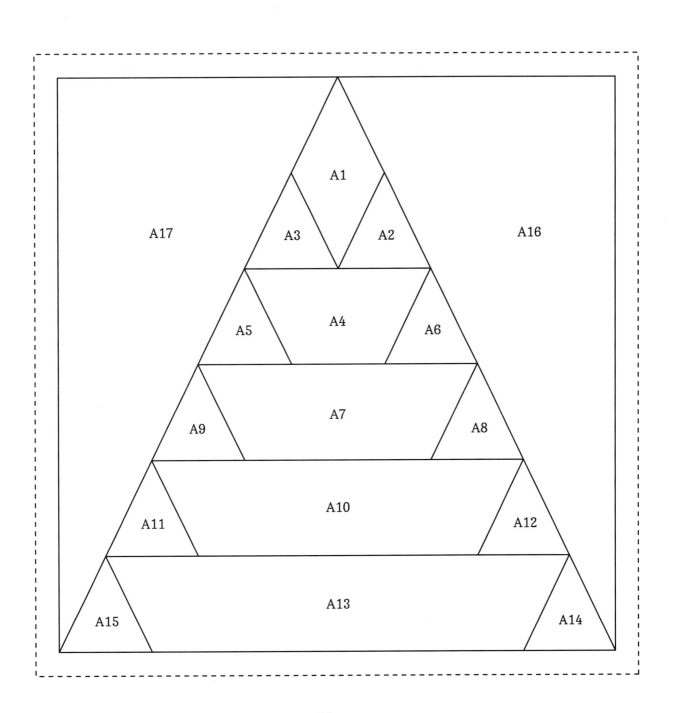

Border

RESOURCES

Paper Piecing Tools:

Add-A-Quarter
Add-An-Eighth
Add-Enough

CM Designs, Inc.
7968 Kelty Trail
Franktown, Colo. 80116
Web: www.addaquarter.com
E-mail: addaqtr@msn.com

Fabric:

Newcastle Fabrics
27 8th Street
Passaic, N.J. 07055
Web: www.newcastlefabric.com
Web: www.newfabs.com
Phone: 973-815-0700 ext. 121

Moda Fabrics
13800 Hutton Drive
Dallas, Texas 75234
Web: www.modafabrics.com
Phone: 800-527-9447

Batting:

The Warm Company
5529 – 186th Place SW
Lynnwood, Wash. 98037
Phone: 425-248-2424

Long Arm Quilters:

Willey Nice Quilts
Carol Willey
Castle Rock, Colo.
Phone: 303-681-0312
E-mail: WilleyNiceQuilts@aol.com

Canterberry Quilting
Susan Bateman
Parker, Colo.
Phone: 720-260-3028
E-mail: canterberryquilting@gmail.com